Joy Before Night

Cover design by Madhu

JOY
Before Night

The Last Years of Evelyn Eaton

By Terry Eaton

*This publication made possible with
the assistance of the Kern Foundation*

**The Theosophical Publishing House
Wheaton, Ill. U.S.A.
Madras, India/London, England**

The Theosophical Publishing House
306 West Geneva Road
Wheaton, IL 60187

A publication of the Theosophical Publishing House, a department of the Theosophical Society in America.

Library of Congress Cataloging-in-Publication Data

Eaton, Terry.
  Joy before night.
    "A Quest book."
    1. Eaton, Evelyn Sybil Mary, 1902-   —Biography—
Last years and death. 2. Authors, American—20th century—
Biography. 3. Healers—United States—Biography. 4. Indians
of North America—Religion and mythology. 5. Indians of
North America—Medicine. 6. Eaton, Terry. I. Title.
PS3509.A84Z64   1988   813'.52 [B]   88-40135
ISBN 0-8356-0634-1 (pbk.)

Printed in the United States of America

Contents

Contents

Foreword

It was the basic humanity of the lady that was so compelling, that struck me so forcibly when, in 1978, I met Evelyn Eaton for the first and only time. When we said hello to each other, I became her immediate close friend. The same was true for most of those who were fortunate enough to come to know her. This was her magic. Here was no self-styled guru. Here was no sobersided mysterious mystic. Here was a lady of good-humored strength with a constant challenging twinkle in her eye; a lady of cosmic perspective about life and the living of life. To the world she became known as "Eve," and surely this sobriquet was most appropriate. For she was a genuine "first lady" to her many, many friends.

How does one put the character, the immortal imprint of such a lady into words? Impossible! About the best that can be done is to invite one who knew her longest and best, one who was her closest physical and spiritual companion, to tell the world about the last years of her mother's physical life. In the process of accomplishing this, Terry Eaton demonstrates that she has indeed inherited the literary genes that made her mother an internationally respected and beloved author. For Terry's lively, at times poignant, stories of Eve's adventures during her closing years on earth do indeed capture the charm and warmth of her spirit; the merriment that was never far beneath the surface of her nature; the depth of travail and the boundless contentment that transcended the travail. From the first to the last page of this loving memorial, *Joy Before Night* captures the compassion that was the heart of Evelyn Eaton, the times of heartfelt satisfaction as Eve reached out to those who were struggling along in our befuddled world. Thus does Terry Eaton, loving daughter and biographer, offer us a sensitive and warm picture of her "life with Eve."

Evelyn Eaton was a theosophist. She was not a member of the Theosophical Society, but rather a participant in the theosophical philosophy. This became immediately apparent when, in 1978, she submitted a manuscript to the Theosophical Publishing House. With her infallible sense of poetic rightness, she called it *I Send a Voice*. In this autobiographical account of her experiences in an Amerindian Sweat Lodge, one finds throughout a strong thread of the perennial wisdom. Here is an affirmation of the brotherhood of all humanity, a confirmation of the oneness—the interdependence—of all creatures. Then too, *I Send a Voice* reveals the author's awareness, and use of, the invisible powers that surround us and influence our lives. Both in this book, and in her subsequent one, *The Shaman and the Medicine Wheel*, Eve demonstrates how one can put these powers to work for the benefit of humankind. With her associates, she "wills" the universal holistic healing power of nature for the use of those in need of assistance. She stresses the essential responsibility of each person to act with love, and affirms the immortality of the human soul. All these ideas and ideals are basic to theosophy. This is why we have been delighted to publish what Eve has had to say, and this is why we are equally delighted to publish Terry Eaton's *Joy Before Night*. It is a blessing to the world that this "daughter of Eve" has been able to capture the essence of her mother's spirit. And it was a great spirit, a spirit that was eloquently expressed in Eve's epilogue to *I Send a Voice*, which goes in part:

> Great Spirit,
> we are blind and deaf.
> Open your eyes in us
> that we may see,
> open your ears in us
> that we may have compassion
> upon the Earth,
> upon our Mother Earth.
>
> Great Spirit,
> When we face the sunset
> when we come singing
> the last song, may it be
> without shame, singing
> "it is finished in beauty,
> it is finished in beauty!"

Clarence Pedersen, former
Publications Manager
for Quest Books

Preface

The title of this book, *Joy Before Night*, comes from
an old superstition about crows. Whenever my
mother saw one she would point it out and say,
"One crow sorrow, watch it out of sight, joy before night." If there happened to be several, she
would recite a slightly longer version:

> One crow sorrow,
> Two crows mirth,
> Three crows a wedding,
> Four crows a birth.
> Five crows silver,
> Six crows gold,
> Seven crows a secret,
>   never to be told.

I don't know where or when I first heard her say
this. It may have been in France, her adopted
country before World War II, and my birthplace. It
could have been in England, where we landed in
1936 to escape the "gathering storm." More likely
it was in Nova Scotia, her father's land, to which
we sailed two years later in separate ships, hers, a
rusty cattle boat, mine the luxury liner Duchess of
York. I was too small at the time to grasp that this
was not the first passage that my mother booked
ahead in order to smooth my course through life,
nor would it be the last.

Wherever we travelled, separately or together, we were often in the company of crows. Magically, one is calling to me at this moment from beyond my city apartment window. I feel compelled to rush out and watch it out of sight, believing completely, much as the child who wishes on a star believes, that much joy will come of it before the day is through.

My affection for crows deepened to reverence when I learned, some time ago, that the Nova Scotia Micmacs, from whom my mother claimed descent, and many other tribes look on crows and ravens as "little black eagles" or messengers to the Grandfathers, who in turn are the mediators to the Great Spirit, the Great Imagination, the Great Mysterious, or—especially pleasing to a writer—the Author of Mankind as some call God.

This book, then, will be my flight with crows over remembered terrain, lighting down now and then on weather-beaten signposts to reflect as best I can the extraordinary impact my mother and her teachings had on me and on my children. A personal perspective of the close ties between us as mother-daughter, mentor-student, and ultimately, as two women bonded together in deep friendship based on mutual love and respect. Two women on the same path and separated only by experience and years.

It will not be a retelling of her life but will focus, rather, on the final months of her journey, highlighting en route, or in crow-fashion, episodes of sorrow, mirth, ceremonies, birth—a little alchemy perhaps?—and even a secret or two that can now be told.

Evelyn Eaton was first and foremost the novelist,

the poet, the pro. Writing was an integral part of her life's mission; she viewed the artist as a highly select standard-bearer whose express responsibility, in whatever chosen media, is to radiate light through creative work.

Many of her books, notably her autobiography, *The Trees and Fields Went the Other Way* (Harcourt Brace Jovanovich), her collection of New Yorker stories (Harper and Row, Farrar and Straus), and the last three personal accounts of her spiritual quest—have already spelled out, in the meticulous language for which she was widely known and admired, the fascinating facts and road maps of her travel through much of the twentieth century. For those, however, for whom this book may be an introduction to the woman whose Indian name means Hands-Show-Way, quotes from a brochure written in 1980 might serve as a sketchy guide.

"To some, Evelyn Eaton is known as 'Grandmother'; to others as author, poet, world traveller, lecturer and teacher. To all who seek contact with her, whether at her home in Independence, California, or on her many travels throughout the country, she is known as a bridge between western and Native American cultures, a sharer of visions, and, as one admirer put it, 'a mystic with a keen sense of humor.'

"We are all contemporaries with different sets of memories, she often told her audiences. Her own set of memories covers an astonishing variety of accomplishments, including twenty-three novels, two short story collections, three volumes of poetry, an autobiography, and scores of articles and essays.

"Born in Switzerland in 1902 to Canadian parents, Evelyn Eaton was educated in England, Canada, and France, where she lived as a struggling young writer until 1936. At age eight her first poem was published in the *Montreal Star*.

"In 1944 she became an American citizen and celebrated her first Fourth of July in Chunking, China, as a war correspondent assigned to cover the China-Burma-India theatre.

"At the war's end, she lived in New York where she continued to write. She was president of the Pen and Brush Club and taught creative writing at Columbia University. Other teaching posts took her to Mary Washington University and Sweet Briar College in Virginia, Ohio State University, Pershing College in Nebraska, and, as its first woman faculty member, to Deep Springs College in California. She is a ten-time Fellow of the MacDowell Colony in Peterborough, New Hampshire, a Fellow of the Virginia Center for Creative Arts, of the Montalvo and Huntington Hartford Foundations in California. She is one of twelve contemporary artists to be selected by Boston University to have her manuscripts and papers in permanent collection at the Mugar Memorial Library.

"Her first encounters with Paiute and Arapaho medicine people date back to 1962 when she first came to the Owens Valley. Since that time she has diligently studied and been trained in Native American spiritual traditions.

"Three books, *Snowy Earth Comes Gliding* (Bear Tribe Publications), and *I Send a Voice*, and *The Shaman and the Medicine Wheel* (both Quest Books) recount her personal experiences as a participant in time-honored rites, ceremonies, Sweat Lodges, and other sacred ways that certain medicine people now feel the time is right "to share with persons sincerely seeking directions to a center for spiritual growth."

After her death in 1983, I wrote to William Shawn, then editor of *The New Yorker*, and described her further:

"She went from horse and carriage days to space shuttles and found it all delightful, exciting, every scrap of it. She kept her childlike awe to the end. She was 80 when she died, she was 16 while she lived. She was wise. She was innocent. She was merry. She was vexed. She was teacher and student emeritus. She loved our Earth Mother with a passion and taught countless others to do the same. She was the greatest supporter of our most fragile dreams. As one friend put it, 'She was never put down by the circumstances of living. There was always something new to be met. She made life such an adventure.' Another, a film producer in Colorado, succinctly summed it up: 'Don't forget she had a great run. Went places, saw things, did things, said things and left her mark as few people have either the talent or energy to do.' "

In sweet irony, Saint Paul may have said it best. My mother was never overly fond of the Apostle to the Romans and Corinthians, although she frequently quoted his admonishments to armor ourselves in the shield of light. "That old bore Saint Paul," she would sigh. "He had some very unsound notions about women. I think he gave us all rather short shrift." But when he wrote, "Be not conformed to this world but be ye transformed by the renewing of your mind," he certainly had her pegged.

My mother was never one to conform to this world nor, I suspect, to any other. And if ever she bore a trademark it was in her continuous, spirited quest and the amaranthine renewing of her mind.

This book is dedicated to Evelyn Eaton in joyous memory. And to my children, Marty, John, David and Rick, who so generously shared their grandmother with all those other "grandchildren."

Chapter One

The night my mother died, or "took off her human envelope" as she called it, the wind swept down from the High Sierra and swirled through the tiny California town of Independence, shaking the cottonwoods that line the streets and sending large clumps of tumbleweed and desert dust to the four directions.

It had begun earlier, as a soft rustling in the leaves of the "live" oaks in my front yard. I had fallen asleep to the sound and to the continual rush of the stream that sped past my small rented trailer in the foothills below what appears to be a Swiss Chalet, but is actually the Mt. Whitney Fish Hatchery.

I was tired that night. I had just returned from a quick trip to San Diego, some 350 miles south. On my way back, I had planned to stop at the house where my mother was recuperating from a massive heart attack, to let her know I was safe (at eighty, she still worried), to present her with a large shell I had found on the shore and to share some good news about a future production a director had asked me to consider.

I knew she would be pleased. She had supported my career in theatre from the time I was four—and was accepted as a company member of le Théâtre du Petit Monde—to the present. She was my most loyal and dedicated fan. She backed me in all the interim jobs as well, what actors call the "in-between challenges" which, since my marriage had dissolved, had covered a variety of underpaid and overworked ventures, mostly in public relations. But no matter how minor the role, my stints on stage were what gave her the greatest satisfaction.

It was late, though, when I drove past, and seeing only a dim light in the window next to her bed, I thought that the news this time could wait, so I continued on to my trailer a few miles up the road.

I knew she would understand. It was the first night in four and a half months that I hadn't either called or stopped to say good night. I would be there first thing in the morning to take over from the young women who had voluntarily arrived a few weeks earlier to assist us in setting up home care. Or possibly from Edie, her friend and companion of the past seven years, whose house we had converted into a hospice.

Indeed, the combined efforts of our care, the healing Sweats and my mother's gallant battle were beginning to pay off. She had been steadily improving, had not required the oxygen tank, was walking occasionally in the garden. She was able to sit up for longer intervals to greet the dozens of

2

well-wishers passing through. She was even talking of starting another book.

So when the phone rang at 1:30 in the morning and Edie said, "She's taken the Swan Boat, Terry. It is finished in beauty," I would not, could not, believe it. "No!" I cried out. "No, no!" I howled, and shot out of the trailer into the yard. "No!" I yelled, and ran in crazy naked circles around the trees. Around and around I tore, until finally, utterly spent, I stopped to lean against the largest oak and cling to its trunk for support.

The wind, stronger now, scraped the branches together and the sound, ricocheting about the yard, tapped an insistent "yes." Above me, the black sky was perforated by brilliant stars. High among them a comet suddenly streaked through the night. Watching its blaze of light I knew at last that it was true. My absurd and solitary cry dance was done.

I stumbled back into the trailer, dressed in whatever I could find, and drove to the house. As I entered I was dimly aware of two or three women whose faces were a blur as they silently passed by me on their way to the kitchen, to leave me in privacy. I went straight to my mother's bed, knelt down beside it and gently touched her forehead, a gesture I had made a thousand times before. Someone had lit candles and shadows flicked across her face.

I stared at those familiar features and my mind whirled as erratically as the wind. All that wisdom, I thought, locked away. All that humor. All that compassion. All that knowledge. I ran my fingers through her soft white hair. "I love you," I said.

3

Eve wearing Hyemeyohsts Storm's cap

"You do know that." I said a good many things; I asked a host of questions. Finally I remembered to say, "Go to the light, Maman, you've earned it."

I half expected her to reach for my hand and squeeze it reassuringly. The shock, which would stay with me for many days, was that she didn't. Couldn't. Not ever again. Not on *this* plane.

Long moments later, the women returned. One by one they hugged me and murmured their sympathies. Someone began a chant. I sat among them, numb, listening to their voices and to the steady rattling of the windows. The wake had begun. But for me, recalling a line from a poem, it was as though all the toys of the world had broken.

I don't remember much about the next three days except for a vague sense of time suspended and much aimless wandering about the garden. I called the children, who were of course devastated. I called their father, who was commiserative and kind. I called Raymond Stone, our long-time friend, the Paiute Medicine Man my mother referred to as Eagle Man in *I Send a Voice*.

Word went out. People came, paid their respects and left. Among the first to arrive was Raymond's "interpreter," a German, whose chance meeting with my mother in Minnesota, in 1968, had led him to move with his family to the Owens Valley and to train under Raymond for years.

The sight of Gunter, and his youngest son, touched something off in me as they stood by my mother's bed to deliver a long prayer in German. As I listened to the cadence of their voices I hoped this eulogy might finally release my mother from a

5

long-held mistrust of the nation which in two world wars had deprived her of her father, husband and many close friends. When Gunter later handed me a broken wheel from a toy truck he had found in the high desert, I saw it as a symbol of her spirit breaking free to dance in the Universal Wheel.

The wind continued to shake the valley. My mother's "envelope" lay undisturbed in the house. The caretakers huddled in corners, talking quietly among themselves, making plans to pick up the lives they had so unselfishly interrupted to be here with the one they called "Grandmother." Edie made calls of her own and valiantly organized meals, lists and busy-work to cover her grief.

Finally, a sage-colored van (I remember thinking how appropriate that it should be this shade) arrived from Los Angeles to take my mother's envelope to the Westwood Crematory.

I was sitting in Edie's front yard when it came. A tall thin man got out and introduced himself as the mortician. A moment later, a tall stocky man, the mortician from Inyo County, pulled up in a long black car. The two men shook hands and walked up to the porch.

My mother had arranged this long before. In her disdain for traditional funerals, the trappings and the expense, she had joined something called the Inyo-Kern Memorial Society, which allowed her to circumvent the things she most abhorred about the methods our society uses to bury its own. We honored her wishes. No fuss, no frills, no embalmment. A simple carrying-off, cremation, then a scattering of her ashes at the appropriate time.

My sharpest memory of that day took place a
few moments later as the morticians waited outside
the house. The front door suddenly flew open and
Edie burst out onto the porch carrying an abalone
shell full of burning sage.

"You can't come in!" she exclaimed in her best
Katharine Hepburn manner (she slightly resembles
the actress), "not until you've smudged yourselves." Puzzled, the men towered above her.
"It's part of our tradition," she added firmly. And
she circled them briskly, fanning the smoke toward
their faces. They eyed each other, shrugged their
shoulders and complied. Once she was satisfied
that they were properly "washed," she allowed
them to follow her into the house.

I stayed in the garden, and for the first time in
three days, I smiled broadly. I knew my mother
must have loved that scene. Two grown men, with
no clue as to what smudging meant, meekly sub-
mitting to Edie's command. Bless her, I thought. I
probably wouldn't have remembered.

A few moments later, one of the men came outside to hand me the death certificate. I signed,
shakily. Now it was official. Now all that remained
was the placing of my mother's body into the van.
They brought her out on a gurney and made the
transfer with quiet efficiency. They closed the
doors, nodded goodbye and prepared to leave, the
black car first, the van following.

To spare me, one of the caretakers had volun-
teered to drive down to Los Angeles and return
with my mother's ashes. (I will always be grateful
to her for that act of kindness. I am grateful to
each one, to Marilyn, Peggy, Theresa, Susan,

Bhagawati, Darsha, Sage, and Selena, for all their days and nights of selfless care, their very important give-away.)

So this is where it ends, I thought, as I followed the van's slow progress up Market Street, past the school and firehouse on one side, the library and courthouse on the other, turning left at Pine's Cafe, past the few familiar landmarks of Independence, down Highway 395 toward Los Angeles.

All the highways and byways of her life—from Europe to Canada, from China to America, from village to town, from city to city—the culmination of ten lifetimes in one—and now this, the earthly goodbye to everything that she had loved most in the region. The majestic mountains, wild streams, rocks, trees, high desert. All the "four-leggeds, wingeds and crawlies" of the valley. The sun rising in the east above the ancient Inyos and setting in the west behind the towering Sierra.

Long after the van had gone, I leaned against a fence post, lost in time, aware only of the hot wind burning my face.

How *had* it come to this?

Chapter Two

It had begun a few months before, in February, with another phone call at 1:30 in the morning. A friend at Esalen, in Big Sur, told me with grave concern that my mother had been taken in the night to a hospital in Monterey. He said he thought it might be a heart attack since she had been having difficulty breathing and was in significant pain. He said that Chris Price, wife of Esalen's director, Dick, had thought it best to get her to a doctor.

How could it be? I wondered, as I groggily took in the details. For several days my mother had been at Esalen on her own, for a much-needed rest and a "spot of fun," as she put it. She had recently completed a whirlwind schedule conducting workshops, travelling from one to the other in the Tioga motor home that Edie, friend, assistant and in this case chauffeur, had bought for just this purpose.

After their final workshop they had wound up in Santa Cruz and were ready to turn home when word reached Edie that due to a family crisis she was urgently needed further north. Not knowing how long she might be detained, Edie suggested dropping my mother off at Esalen while she took care of the matter, and returning for her as soon as she could. My mother jumped at the chance. She was so rarely alone these days and Esalen was one of her favorite places. She had been there on several occasions as a leader but seldom as a guest. She looked forward to having some free time to soak in the hot tubs (fed by the same natural hot springs the original Esalen tribe had considered sacred), and to the good organically-grown food, body massages and the personal attentions of a doting staff.

I had already received a postcard from her—a picture of a sea otter lying blissfully on its back in the Pacific Ocean—with the message "*Exactly* how I feel. And probably look. I'm being thoroughly pampered and I love it. Such wicked luxury!"

My friend's voice broke through my thoughts.

"Someone will call you from the hospital," he told me. "I thought I should prepare you. Sorry to have to wake you with such bad news."

I thanked him and went unsteadily back to bed. There was nothing I could do until morning except pray, which I did, long and hard, and try to sleep.

The call from the hospital came at six.

"How soon can you get here?" It was the night nurse, who had been on duty when my mother was brought in. "She's had a severe heart attack. She's in critical condition."

"It will take me about eight hours," I told her. "I need to make a few arrangements and then I'll be on my way as fast as possible."

10

"Good," she answered, "because she's been calling for you. I'll tell her you're coming. I know this will comfort her."

I immediately phoned my son David in San Diego, who made emergency plans to drive to Monterey. I notified the other grandchildren, John in Indiana, Marty in Kansas, and as Rick had no phone, I left messages with friends of his in Ridgecrest, where he lived.

I hurriedly threw some clothes in my duffle bag and drove to my mother's house in Independence, the small redwood bungalow she shared with Iren Marik, the Hungarian concert pianist she had met and befriended at Sweet Briar College in 1950. My mother's admiration and respect for Iren's brilliant talent had led her to found the Deepest Valley Concert Series, which were held in the natural amphitheatre of the Alabama Hills, high above Lone Pine.

Iren flew out from Virginia for five summers in a row, beginning in 1965, to give these spectacular concerts in that prehistoric setting which my mother described in full detail in *The Trees and Fields Went the Other Way*. When it came time for Iren to retire from the college, my mother invited her to *think* about moving permanently to California and sharing the house. Iren and her piano arrived simultaneously.

In 1978 Charles Hillinger of the *Los Angeles Times* described them in a long article as the "Independents from Independence."

"The two of them are indomitable, like the towering snow-shrouded High Sierra looming majestically over their modest home," he wrote, adding,

11

Deepest Valley concert in Alabama Hills, Lone Pine, California

"Together, in their twilight years, sharing the expenses of maintaining a home, but each fiercely independent, Evelyn Eaton in the study where she works on her latest manuscript four hours every morning, seven days a week, Iren Marik in her studio where she plays her Steinway Concert D piano six hours a day, seven days a week." He further described their daily routines, their individual philosophies, and went on to state that on the first Tuesday of every month their home became a concert hall for—as he put it—"one of Iren's memorable performances" and, on every Monday, an open house for "stimulating discussions. 'We talk about everything under the sun, anything that comes to mind—the new era, Indians, Tibetan Lamas...' said Evelyn. 'Young and old, men and women from all over the valley drop in on us on Monday evenings. It's great fun. Iren plays her music'."

At the end of his article, Hillinger noted, "Their energies and talents are boundless. They are remarkable."

It was not entirely an idyllic situation. The fact that they did practice different disciplines, and yet respected one another's fields, was what saved their often difficult friendship from potential disaster.

In temperament they were diametric opposites. While my mother generally shied like a frightened rabbit from anything resembling a confrontation, Iren was not one to suffer most people gladly, let alone fools. And though her deep Hungarian bark was infinitely worse than her bite, not many people learned to appreciate the difference if, as was

13

often the case, Iren took a dislike to their politics, religion, sex, race, looks or whatever else might set her off momentarily. Visitors were often startled and somewhat abashed by her greeting, "*Must* you stay? *Can't* you go?"

The few on whom this lesson was not lost, however, were rewarded by her fierce loyalty, generosity, magnanimity and wildly extravagant Hungarian chocolate cake. I was one of the lucky ones, but it called for diplomacy—a careful balancing act. When I slipped, I took my lumps with the rest.

With this in mind, I broke the news of my mother's condition as gently as I could. Even so, her immediate response was, "What *utter* nonsense! You *don't* know what you say." It was one time, certainly, that I wished she had been right. Nevertheless, she insisted on sending me off with cold chicken, fresh coffee, fruit and something delectably sweet, and my promise that I would call her the moment I arrived.

I drove at top speed over Tehachapi Pass, through the oil fields of Bakersfield, up Interstate 5, across to 101, praying aloud, bargaining and pleading with the Grandfathers as the road stretched endlessly on and heavy rain pelted the roof of my small pickup truck. I reached the hospital parking lot at the same time as David did, and together we ran towards the main entrance, ducking our heads against a torrential downpour. Inside, distraught and wet, we hugged each other for a long moment and then quickly went to find David's "Gran."

She was in the intensive care unit, in a dimly-lit room, lying on a slightly elevated bed and

14

swamped by seemingly hundreds of tubes extending from her arms, nose and mouth. Nearby, a monitor tracked her damaged heartbeats across a small screen.

Her face was grey and drawn, her eyes were closed, but as we neared her bed she opened them slightly and in spite of being heavily sedated, she managed a weak smile of recognition.

"We're here," we told her, and she nodded slowly and smiled again.

We sat quietly next to the bed as she drifted in and out of sleep. After a while a nurse ushered us into the adjoining room.

"She's had a bad time," she told us. "But now that you're here I'm sure we'll see an improvement. The next few days will tell. They're the critical ones." She patiently answered my many questions and told me I could talk to the physician in the morning. It was a relief to hear that he was considered one of the top heart specialists in the area.

Once she assured me that she would keep a close watch through the night, the nurse advised us to get some rest and then, as an afterthought, handed me two phone messages from Esalen.

After one more glance through the door window David and I blew silent kisses to the sleeping form and went to the lobby to make the calls.

I dialed the first number. Chris Price answered. It was she who had brought my mother to the hospital, driving with a friend through slashing rain along that dark and isolated road while my mother clung precariously to life. She filled in more details of the harrowing trip and then suggested, although she knew we must be tired, that David and I come to Esalen for the night to pick up my mother's belongings. She was concerned that the road conditions would worsen and access might soon be impossible. (She was right. A few days later Highway 1 was completely shut off to traffic due to terrible landslides.)

"Has anyone notified Edie?" I asked.

"Yes, I did. This afternoon. She'll be there tomorrow."

I thanked her for her help, then I put in a quick call to Iren. I told her all I could, that it was serious and that she should pray hard. Iren had been a devout Catholic until the liturgy was changed from Latin to English. In protest, she never went to Mass again. "Teruska," she said, using the pet name she had for me when she was genuinely concerned for my welfare, "I will pray. I will even write to the Pope."

We returned to intensive care and told the nurse our plans. "Might as well go while you can," she said. "She's fairly stable now and it will comfort her to have her things."

We left in David's car, not saying much as we drove, both of us near exhaustion. It was a long difficult trip, but at last we turned down the steep entrance to Esalen. Chris was waiting for us in the main hall. She had saved supper for us and after we had eaten with little appetite, she led us outside to Unit 16, which had been my mother's room.

We said good night at the door, then, getting out of our wet clothes, we chose beds and quickly settled in. A sweet smell of sage permeated the room.

16

Outside, the sound of waves crashing along the shore mingled with the clatter of rain on the roof.

"Grandfathers, Grandmothers. Please," I prayed. "I thank you for all the courtesies you show us and for all our blessings. Be with her tonight. Stand guard over her. Let no more harm come to her."

In the morning, waking to grey mist and still more rain, we packed my mother's possessions, assorted books, stones, shells, sweet grass, sage, medicine objects, clothes and other personal items. Only one thing seemed to be missing, and that was her walking stick, the one Paul Brenner, physician and author of *Life Is a Shared Creation*, had meticulously carved for her some months before, and from which she had seldom been separated since he had brought and presented it to her. We made a thorough search but to this day its whereabouts remains a mystery.

We carried everything else to the car. Taking one last sweep of the room, I noticed a piece of paper on the small desk by the doorway on which someone had hurriedly thrown together a paragraph or two releasing Esalen from all liability. My mother's wobbly signature was at the bottom. I left it where it was, my silent reproach to whoever had (heartlessly, I thought) in the midst of my mother's extreme pain, exacted this pledge.

As soon as everything had been packed, we headed back, adroitly avoiding the large boulders that had crashed to the road during the night.

We reached the hospital a few minutes before ten, in time to meet the physician in the small visitors' lounge a few steps from intensive care. I

17

liked him on sight. He had a good, strong face and intelligent eyes. He used long medical terms to describe the type of attack she had suffered, and then he explained, gently, that the prognosis was not the best. But, he told us, he had seen worse cases pull through and he was guardedly optimistic.

"Your mother and I have discussed the possibility of a pacemaker," he said. "I guess it's no surprise to you that she's adamantly against it. That, and all other life support systems. I just want you to know I will honor her request. I can tell she's an exceptional lady with a mind of her own. I hope I can get to know her better when she's stronger."

If this *had* to have happened, I thought to myself, thank you for sending her to a humane and compassionate man. He went on to describe her medications and then, after shaking our hands, he left for his appointed rounds. The room seemed lighter somehow, though the skies outside were as dark as pewter.

Memory warps my sense of time. Fourteen days spent uneventfully at one's job, in rehearsal, in the running of one's family, the hours go by at a comfortable clip. Two weeks at a hospital and time lengthens to the pace of a lumbering giant tortoise. Step. Pause. Step. I look back at the Monterey interval as one of the longest stretches of my life. Yet, in spite of a blurred recollection, a few scenes still flit through my mind like the Nova Scotia fireflies I used to capture in glass jars on summer nights.

Edie arrived. David left, taking my love and gratitude on his long trek home. Due to his big heart and to his living within close range, it has been his lot to see me through some of my more difficult times.

Because my mother had already touched them, the hospital staff relaxed the rules, allowing Edie to keep her Tioga parked at the back of the hospital and both of us to come and go at will. In the beginning, we alternated our nights of vigil at my mother's bed. When we felt it safer, we spent our nights tucked away in the Tioga, sheltered from the gusty downpour, talking about and planning my mother's future care in Independence.

But that was later. Before, in all our anxious scurryings back and forth, my mother serenely surrendered to the regimen of her doctor, nurses, IVs, pills, shots, orderlies, trays, bed-pans, loudspeakers and monitors. More important, she had privately submitted to the Divine Will, knowing that help was being sent through other channels.

On one particularly bumpy night when she suddenly spiked a fever, I put in a call to Raymond Stone. He went to work at once. He told me to take hold of her left hand in a certain way and not to let go until I knew the "time is right," no matter what happened.

I followed his instructions. I held her hand and began to chant one of Raymond's songs, the one he had said to use. Almost at once, I felt an electric charge course through me, what my son John, when he was little and excited about something, used to call "ginger ale in my toes."

19

Eagle man Paiute

It may have been only minutes or hours, in the timeless way these things happen, but her fever subsided and she rested peacefully. I called Raymond in the morning to thank him. "Don't thank *me*," he said, "Thank the Helpers above."

Above, below, side by side, they were all there, the seen and the unseen. Gradually, gradually, her heart began to repair. In time, she was moved from intensive care to a private room. In time, the nurses had her shakily on her feet, walking slowly around the room. In time, she was complaining about the food. In time, she had us all laughing again.

Her hospital stay happened to coincide with the visit of England's Queen Elizabeth and Prince Phillip to California. They were sailing up the coast from San Diego to San Francisco, but the heavy rains had forced them to anchor off Monterey temporarily.

"How considerate of them to come, and all this way," my mother said when we told her they were so close by. "But I can't possibly receive them here. I do hope they'll understand. Another time perhaps." She sank back against her pillow and smiled, recalling aloud how, as a young woman, she had been presented at the court of Elizabeth's grandmother, Queen Mary. "Though just in case," she added with a wink, "do be a lamb and fetch me a clean nightgown."

Flowers and plants began to arrive by the dozens. In one of her typical give-aways, she instructed the nurses to deliver these to other patients. The ones, she emphasized, who didn't seem to have any visitors. Let them be from

20

whomever they imagined: an old love, a child, a secret admirer, someone to whom they had mattered.

Soon bundles of cards, letters and telegrams were brought to her room. And while, as always, she had difficulty believing so many people cared, the volume of mail gave her great pleasure. She had me list all who had written so that she could answer each one personally. "When I get *home*," she said, fixing me with a determined look.

Chapter Three

Home. On the day she was released, with doctors, nurses and patients along the halls waving affectionate goodbyes, I took off ahead in much higher spirits and noticed for the first time that the rain had stopped. My mother followed in the Tioga, which Edie drove slowly and carefully over scenic routes and back roads. They made one stop in San Jose to be checked by my mother's great good friend, Dr. G., a Buddhist healer who had been keeping close tabs on her progress by phone.

I arrived in Independence in time to prepare Iren for the decision we had already made to move my mother into Edie's house temporarily. Located next door, it was more conveniently arranged, and, I added tactfully, my mother being there would mean fewer interruptions of Iren's daily practice at the piano. Iren was not at all pleased with this plan until my mother's arrival a day or two later, when she could see for herself her old friend's weakened condition.

Iren's own health was not the best. Over the years she had developed severe arthritis and walking was difficult and painful. The long hours she managed to put in at the piano were a source of constant amazement, though we knew that music was her life. She said as much daily. And so it was—right to the end. But it was a life that brooked little interference with her rigid schedule. So, to have my mother safely ensconced next door, yet within walking distance, seemed the most reasonable solution.

During the first weeks of my mother's recuperation Edie and I took turns being on duty, spelled occasionally by Marilyn Mountain and Peggy Howard, two of my mother's "starling" students who at the time lived in Independence.

My mother's bed was placed in the living room next to the front window, through which she could look at the snowcapped mountains reflecting the rays of the early spring sun.

The room was bright and cheery, the antithesis of a hospital. We spent long hours in it, reading aloud, talking quietly, fixing meals, and when she slept, writing letters on her behalf.

Initially sleep came in long stretches. Later it was fitful and her waking hours were largely at night. It was then that she wanted to talk, to be reassured, to reassure. And while we welcomed these intimate and philosophical conversations, laced with her own brand of humor, our having to stay awake throughout the nights as well as during the days began to take a physical toll on us. It soon became clear that we would need more help.

A call went out. Five young women responded. Two arrived almost at once, and in a few days another, and then two more. Their arrival made it

Eve, Edie, and Iren near site of Deepest Valley concerts

possible to set up shifts of two, to alternate days and nights and to give ourselves longer rest periods in-between, though even on our "off" days we were never far from her door.

There was a lot of work involved. Helping her from her bed to her chair without disconnecting her from the oxygen tank took many stops and starts before we perfected the system. Preparing meals (largely Iren's territory), keeping well-meaning but tiring visitors at bay in the early days, washing her hair and changing her clothes were just a few of our tasks. When breathing was difficult, we soothed her fears, joking kindly on the rare occasions when, as a normal side effect of her medications and all that she'd been through, her spirits flagged and she got depressed.

My mother had always been a modest, private person. To have her daughter hovering about, monitoring her consumption of food and pills (and elimination of the same) was, in an unfamiliar role reversal, a necessary nuisance she overcame with sighs of resignation. To have complete strangers ministering to her in the same fashion was, at first, almost more than she could bear. Eventually she got used to the rhythm of our comings and goings and handled "all this fussing about" with dignity and humor.

In the weeks to follow she began to take a more personal interest in her caretakers and in the "tools" she felt each one could develop to help in her healing.

One had a pure, sweet voice and was designated "the singer." One was a physical therapist and was called upon to give long, soothing body rubs. Another had knowledge of the healing properties of certain crystals, and she periodically worked these over my mother's "overcoat." I brought my autoharp to play some favorite tunes: "Amazing Grace," Cole Porter, Old English folk songs and French ditties she had taught me long ago. Iren hobbled over with trays of food and cassettes on which she had recorded piano pieces she especially wanted my mother to hear and that my mother recognized as another source of healing. Edie read aloud from loved and familiar books. In this way we contributed our best talents to her recovery and watched them take effect.

On a surprise visit, after several weeks had passed, a Hopi leader, staying only a few minutes, gave my mother a blessing, and then, taking me aside in the garden before he left, said, "This is good. This is how we used to do for our Elders. It does my heart good to see this. We should always honor and respect the old ones, they have so much to teach us."

It reminded me of something I had heard another leader say at a gathering in northern California a year before, "Always think four times before you cross the path where an Elder has walked. The grass grows back so sweetly where they've been."

I had been so struck by this at the time, and by the sight of my mother walking slowly away from a stage where she had been asked to speak at the same gathering, with her grandson, Rick, at one side and her talking stick for support on the other,

that I wrote a poem for her eightieth birthday com-
memorating this event:

> Four times think
> before you cross
> behind your elders or before—
> for the grass springs back
> more sweetly in their wake.
>
> Oh my mother. Grandmother
> to my four.
> I watch your stately march
> to that place of surrender—
> the gold-west hill,
> still warm in the hint
> of a fading star.
> I see you—
>   at my distance—
> painted stick in hand.
> The hem of your dress
> feathers the ground
> as you move
>   in rhythm
> to the ancient tunes.
>
> And the lonely heart beats time,
> drums its rune of love
> for the grasses where those feet
> have danced.
> For the places of young light,
> for the cliffs of greener songs.
> For the craters of strong winds,
> summer lightning. Storms.

All pilgrim paths and waterways
from which you've spun:
North, East and South
    to West my mother,
Rainbow to my suns.

For her part, my mother talked privately and collectively to us about her deep-seated convictions
and her awareness of our mission in life. She used
the long hours to give us refresher courses in
much of the material she had covered in her books
and at first hand.

We began each day with the ritual of smudging,
or burning sage as incense, covering ourselves four
times with the smoke. For the four directions and
the four H's—humility, honesty, harmony and
humor. Armed with these images and washed
clear of what she called "dross," we could be better prepared to meet the "startles of the day."
Most of which are of our own making, she reminded us, patiently repeating her theory that
many people are young souls at the kindergarten
level in the Creator's plan for humanity. Some of
us have graduated to higher levels, but all of us
have lessons to complete, homework to do and a
curriculum to cover, before we can move on to
postgraduate courses.

She believed in reincarnation, and a theory that
if in past lives we *chose* to sleep through class, we
are given another chance—summer school, as it
were, to repeat the lesson, learn it well and move
on.

We talked of walking in balance on our Earth
Mother, of remembering and honoring the inter-

28

connectedness of all sentient beings. "We must not go on being greedy, corrupt, taking, taking, always taking, without a thought to giving back. How does the song go? 'She's been waiting/She's been waiting so long./She's been waiting for her children to remember to return.' The whole point is to *remember* and return. How does the rest of it go?" We finished it for her: "Blessed be and blessed are/the lovers of the lady/Blessed be and blessed are/the maiden, mother, crone./Blessed be and blessed are/the ones who dance together./Blessed be and blessed are/the ones who dance alone."

She loved that particular song. She knew it by heart, so her ruse of pretending to forget the words was as much her way of getting us to sing it to ourselves as it was to have it sung for her. She wanted us to understand it, to absorb its messages and symbols. Mother Earth patiently waiting. The Goddess. The important transitions in a woman's life—maiden, mother, crone. Each as hallowed and as important as the other and the lessons we gain while we slowly travel through one phase to the next. The viable signs, everywhere, when we do remember to return. Dancing together, dancing alone. An image of mystical nights under long-ago full moons. The Druids, Stonehenge, all the circles and cycles of past and present lives. "It's all part of being in the Army of Light," she would tell us. "Dancing—one should never stop dancing—singing, making offerings, joining full circle."

In her own dance of life she had gleefully learned the Charleston and the Black Bottom in her flapper days, and she could waltz with the best. I vividly remember watching her waltz with Chungliang Al Huang, the Chinese-American T'ai Chi master, whom she had met when she was nearly eighty and who was enchanted by her book on China, *Go Ask the River*. They whirled as gracefully about the perimeter of a large meeting room at Esalen as one imagines lovers danced to the "Skater's Waltz" in Vienna long ago. And then, of course, her own rhythmic progression around ceremonial wheels and the Native American dances she took part in from time to time.

But it was the Medicine Wheel to which she was particularly attracted. In travels to various gatherings, especially those sponsored by the Bear Tribe in 1981 and 1982, but also years before, as she describes in *Snowy Earth Comes Gliding*, she had been made more and more aware of the significance of Medicine Wheels, and their power to counter the reckless acts of the "destroyers." She was convinced and wanted to convince others that, properly used, these wheels could serve to restore health and harmony to Mother Earth.

"We have to understand that our planet is a sentient being, capable of being wounded and hurt when we are discourteous and treat her badly. We must remember to make offerings, to thank our mother, to use the Medicine Wheel as a way of symbolically returning all the gifts and benefits she has provided us with from the very beginning."

This vision of hers had prompted a group of us in the summer of 1982 to lay out a Medicine Wheel in a special area, a grove of ancient oak trees high in the Sierra range between Lone Pine and Independence. We gathered large and small rocks from other regions, making an offering for each one we removed, and again, as we placed each one in its new position. It took two full days to set out the stones, starting at the east, working our way around to the south, west, and north, then placing the "spokes" to the center. Beneath each stone we placed tokens of the mineral world as our offering and our acknowledgment of the heavy damage we have inflicted in our excessive removal of minerals and ore. When we had finished, we joined hands around the outer edge and moved sunwise in a slow dance of celebration. We sang, we chanted, we laughed, we wept.

Four of us had been assigned to "speak" to the "four direction" rocks. We prayed to the East, symbolizing the spring of our lives, new beginnings, a new dawn, the Eagle Messenger, rebirth. To the South, our summer and the place of innocence, joy, children, green and growing things. To the West, or autumn, the place of the Thunder-beings, of surrender, of reflection, maturity and wisdom. To the North, our winter and the place of healing winds and cleansing snows, of truth, courage, strength and the completion of the cycle before its reemergence in the East.

We represented all ages, from a three-month-old baby riding happily around in his mother's backpack, to young adults, middle-agers and elders. There were as many types as ages. Buddhist, Native American, Episcopalian, Catholic, Jew. And all colors. Each of us at our place on the Wheel just as we are, with no position having more im-

31

portance than any other—as it was in the days of King Arthur and as it is today in sacred circles of every sort, from Sweat Lodges to fire-rings.

We spoke of this as we circled around. And as we circled the stones seemed to settle into the ground and to look as though they had been in place for centuries.

At the close of the ceremony my mother—who had sat apart from us, resting her back against a large boulder as she watched the circle-dance and the proceedings—said with some emotion, "You have just made an old woman very happy."

"Two old women," someone piped up. "You and Mother Earth."

"Blessed be," my mother said, and in the next breath, "now what about some ice cream? Is anyone hungry besides me?"

We drifted away from the wheel to a grove with picnic tables, where we ended the day with good food, light conversation, and more songs. When the stars appeared, we went our separate ways down the long mountain road to our homes.

Chapter Four

A few days later, my mother and I sat together in
her writing room, talking and reminiscing about
the wheel, the magic that had taken place among
the trees and the mix of people.

The sun shone through the stained glass windows she had rescued from her grandfather's
home in Fredericton, New Brunswick, several years
before, the same charming windows that her
grandfather had designed especially for his wife
and had ordered from England in 1870. On one
there was the bluebird of happiness and a sym-
bolic pine branch. On another, the English lion
and a large "A. R." for "Archibald FitzRandolph."
Five in all, each casting a warm light on the rows
of books on her shelves and on the collection of
rocks, shells, crystals, family pictures and pages of
her current manuscript on the desk.

My mother sat in her swivel chair, her back to
the view of the garden with its fruit trees and
multicolored roses. I perched comfortably across
from her on the window seat. Spread between us
on the floor was the Navajo rug on which she so

often sat cross-legged to smoke her Pipe and ask for a blessing on her work.

As always, the room was full of the good, sweet smell of sage and a sense of friendly ghosts, characters she had created on her ancient typewriter or snippets of countless conversations we had shared over the years.

"Tell!" she would say at such times, fixing me with her intelligent dark eyes and leaning forward to grasp my hands.

"What do you want to hear?"

"Everything! Tell all."

And that would be the signal to blurt out whatever happened to be on my mind at the moment. The studio was a safe haven for any topic; my children, work, worries, hopes, fears, loves, old and new paths. Often, after a high occasion, we would pick over the finer points of the experience, combining her writer's eye and ear with my often exaggerated sense of drama, exploding into raucous laughter now and then, like school girls sharing the silliest of secrets, and quickly recovering, if we thought anyone was within earshot. Laughter of the sort we generated was often misinterpreted by others as a mark of not taking ourselves "seriously." *But my mother was never more serious than when she was laughing.* It was part of her fierce creed. To make someone laugh each day was holy. And if that couldn't be managed, then we should laugh at ourselves.

Since on this particular day we were reliving the Medicine Wheel, I brought up a past experience with a "Wheel" of a similar nature, though I hadn't known the connection at the time.

34

It had happened ten years before, in 1972, when I had flown to Washington, D. C., to take part in a peace gathering called "Ring-Around-Congress" that had been organized by Joan Baez. I had written about the incident in my journal, and as I now had this with me, I read it aloud, a full description of that particular march on the Capitol whose express purpose, in contrast to the clamor of past demonstrations, had been to form a human chain to circle the capitol buildings and silently pray for peace. It was an early example of the potential of such wheels to bring about healing change, however slowly, and my mother wholeheartedly agreed. And this was a healing in itself, as we had been briefly and uncomfortably polarized during those turbulent days.

Now we sat in companionable silence which my mother broke after a while to speak of her dream of overseeing future Wheels. These would represent the animal and vegetable kingdoms, and would provide more channels of healing help to our Mother Earth. And to ourselves in the process. Her heart attack prevented this. But throughout the days and nights of convalescence she exhorted us to continue the work, with or without her.

During this time one of the caretakers had crafted a miniature Medicine Wheel by carefully gluing a circle of small and colorful pebbles to a piece of cardboard and placing this on a wooden tray. At opposite corners she had drawn a swan and a wolf. My mother spent many hours with this tray on her lap, visualizing help for herself and for any others who may have asked, using the wolf and swan on these occasions as her totems.

35

"Of myself I can do nothing, but with Thy indwelling presence all things are possible."

In the same period, a young woman—a friend and master weaver of fine cloths and wools who lived in Independence—brought a reversible vest she had designed for my mother. On one side, which was cream-colored, she had painstakingly embroidered the silhouette of a swan. On the reverse side, which was a deep maroon shade, she had fashioned the figure of a white wolf with dark brown eyes looking straight ahead.

Without consulting one another, these two women had come up with the same symbols at the same time. I have both the tray and vest in a corner of my bedroom, and I can seldom look at them without recalling my mother's joy in these gifts, and her kinship with the swan and wolf, or for that matter her affinity with birds and animals of every sort. From the hummingbird to the red-tailed hawk, the stray kitten to the mountain lion, she understood our interdependency and the harmony we could achieve when we learn to respect all living things and their place on the Great Wheel. " 'And man shall have dominion' doesn't mean we have the right to destroy life," she would say. "It means we must be *responsible* for what St. Francis called 'our lesser brothers.' "

Yet she admitted that the truth of this had come to her fairly late in life. One unexpected and somewhat startling episode that bore this out took place a few days after she had been presented with the vest and small wheel. I had come to the house early in the morning and had found her sitting on the edge of her bed, looking quite forlorn. "I'm so

36

glad you're here," she said as I walked toward her. "There's something you must do for me, quickly."

In the night, she told me, she had dreamed about a porcupine and, on waking, had been haunted by the memory of what she called "a mean act" she had committed against one of those prickly creatures. It had happened years before when she lived in Quaker Hill, an isolated community in New York State. She had caught sight of a porcupine eating some fruit from one of her apple trees. She had stared at it for a long time, then, on impulse, she had marched into her house (a cottage built in 1776 that was the setting for her book *Give Me Your Golden Hand*), had grabbed a pistol from under her bed, and had stomped back to shoot the hapless animal, right there and then.

I couldn't imagine her ever having done something like that, but she swore to me now that it was true. She wanted to make amends. She asked me to go and create an "apology" ceremony for her as soon as possible. I promised her I would and drove back to my trailer.

I found a secluded spot near the stream where someone had conveniently left an old rubber tire. In its center I placed bits of fruit, nuts, sage and other things I imagined a porcupine might enjoy, though I know very little about them. Then, with all the dignity I could muster, I performed a slow dance around the rim and sang what I hoped would be a suitably melancholy song, asking forgiveness and a blessing on all porcupines. A crow flew over as I sang, and a squirrel chattered nervously from a nearby tree. When I had finished, I

37

drove back to report what I had done. "Oh thank God," my mother said, and smiled in obvious relief.

It was shortly after this that I also had a dream in which a porcupine played a part. The principal role, however, belonged to a small, blue-eyed, tiger-striped cat, Brigit, named for the Celtic Goddess of poetry and poets.

Brigit had come to me a year earlier in a most precarious state. My mother and Edie had found her in the middle of a country road late at night, on one of their return trips from a workshop. The headlights of the Tioga had picked out the small squashed blob of fur, and believing the animal dead, they stopped to remove it from the road, bless and give it a proper burial. As they approached, it startled them by letting out a pitiful sound.

They carefully picked up the little cat, transferred it to the Tioga, wrapped it in a soft towel and drove off to try and find a veterinarian to put it out of its misery. But they were miles from the nearest town and had little hope of finding a clinic open at that hour. As they talked this over, my mother noticed that the kitten seemed to be recovering ever so slightly.

They stopped again. This time my mother sent a "voice" to the Grandfathers and asked for help. When she was done, she took some milk from the small refrigerator at the back of the Tioga, warmed it on the propane stove and placed it in a saucer in front of the tiny animal. Slowly and painfully the kitten crawled out from under the towel and weakly lapped at the milk. Then it suddenly purred.

That was the deciding factor. As soon as they reached home, they brought her up to my trailer in a shoebox. They later confessed they were counting on my weakness for dogs and cats to get me to agree to keep her. I already had Rocky, a large copper-colored (blue-eyed also) Siberian Husky, but I accepted this new responsibility the moment I saw her.

Miraculously, Rocky accepted her too. Ordinarily, moving objects of any size—I had seen him go after large deer—were fair game and sometimes, alas, a meal. But from Brigit he kept a respectful distance and in time, when the last of her many scars had healed, I frequently found her curled up in contented sleep against his side or right below his large head, oblivious to any possible danger.

In my dream, Brigit had somehow or other managed to collect a veritable zoo of animals and birds and had herded them into my yard. From there she organized a long parade, leading this contingent of creatures—ducks, squirrels, badgers, coyote, one large turtle, the porcupine and Rocky, plus a host of hummingbirds, hawks, owls and crows hovering overhead—down the steep mountain road onto the main highway, through the town of Independence straight to my mother's door.

I woke at this point, sorry for the interruption. I had been thoroughly enjoying this quixotic, colorful march and Brigit's take-charge behavior. But now, fully awake, I could hardly wait to report this to my mother before it faded, knowing the importance she placed on dreams. A poem of hers which she had written as a young woman in Paris ends

39

with the lines: ''What outlives us is a dream/And what we dream, reality.''

I drove down the same route the ''parade'' had so recently travelled just as the morning sun broke sharply over the Inyo Mountains and cast dramatic pink shadows among the canyons. My mother, already sitting in the chair next to her bed, brightened when I burst into the room.

''Guess what!' she said, kissing me lightly on the cheek as I leaned down. ''I've just had the most extraordinary experience. I woke up very early, before anyone else, and heard a loud noise outside. I looked out the window and saw all sorts of little animals and birds out there.'' She pointed to the front garden. ''They've all gone now, but wasn't it sweet of them to put in appearance like that!'' She paused, and then added, her voice drifting off, ''Of course, it could have been a dream...''

Chapter Five

Not every waking, or for that matter sleeping, minute was taken up with such momentous events. There were certain "off" days when my mother's strength deteriorated, and she understandably craved solitude. We tried to accomodate her at those times by keeping a respectful distance while still remaining within earshot.

Toward the end of May it seemed to her that she had hit an impasse. She felt she wasn't making much progress physically, although we could see daily improvement. "Everything feels grey and sticky inside," she told me, "like some dark, oppressive swamp. This isn't going the way I imagined. I thought I would be much better by now."

I reminded her how short a time it had been since her attack. "I know," she sighed, "but if this is how I'm going to feel, I'm not sure recovering is worth it. I think it's time for one of my tours."

Long before her illness she had talked about setting up something called "Terminal Tours," her tongue-in-cheek solution for how "loved ones," suspected of being near the end, could sign up for a prepaid cruise or first-class journey to any place they had always wanted to see before they died. Relatives, friends and lovers would then see them off with large baskets of fruit, champagne, much hullabaloo and fond farewells, and this would be the last memory on either side as the "beloved" sailed, flew or rode off into the proverbial sunset.

After seeing Lohengrin at the San Francisco Opera and being charmed by the final progression across the stage, her choice for the journey was the Swan Boat. It became her metaphor. "You have swan songs in the theatre," she pointed out. "I have a swan boat. That's what I intend to go off in. Can't you just see me? Borne away by all those Whistling Swans, and me, nodding and bowing like Queen Mary, on swan's down in the back."

I could but not yet. It was time to seek additional help. I called Raymond Stone and he came that night.

On my mother's bedside table were copies of *The Letters of The Scattered Brotherhood*, a small red leather-bound volume of *The Liturgy of The Liberal Catholic Church*, *Earth Wisdom* by Dolores La Chapelle, *The Education of Little Tree* by Forest Carter (a favorite read-aloud), E. B. White's *The Trumpeter Swan*, A Dorothy Sayer detective book, a well-worn *Oxford Book of Verse*, the White Eagle series and an Alfred Hitchcock magazine.

Among these lay a green spiral notebook in which the caretakers and I solemnly recorded what medicines she had taken when, the food she had eaten that day, all her "roadside business," and reminders to one another about various household

Raymond Stone, Medicine Man (Photo by Louise Kelsey)

tasks. When Raymond arrived, he picked the note-book up and read it with much amusement.

"How you gonna put down the medicine *I* give her?" he teased, and tossed the notebook back on the table with a gesture that implied: you people, you're pretty crazy.

How indeed. Raymond made four visits to the house. He came at night with his "interpreter" and his doctoring tools. He positioned himself at the head of the bed, dwarfing the small figure that lay on it, and smiling down at his old friend "Missus Eaton," he began his work.

His powerful chants filled the room. Etched in that face which so strongly resembles an eagle's—with its high cheekbones, deep-set eyes above a beak-shaped nose and the slightly protruding lower lip—are all the acts of kindness and healing he has performed over the years.

Between his chants he prayed aloud in his own language and performed slow, spellbinding dances about the room, calling on the "helpers" of his country to come to my mother's side. When he had finished, he put his medicine objects away in the small green suitcase my mother had given him years before, said good night, and drove away in his old worn pickup to Big Pine, twenty-six miles away.

The "house calls," as he called them, came a few days apart, and on the fourth and final visit he brought his wife Evalina with him. Those who have seen the pictures of this kind, stalwart woman in *Snowy Earth Comes Gliding* will know the healing strength she brought in consort with Ray-mond's. Evalina belongs to a fundamentalist

44

church which holds its services on the reservation in Big Pine at the same time Raymond conducts Sweat, and while they may seem poles apart in ministries, Evalina's belief is as sincere and devout as Raymond's is. Disparate methods, same source.

At the end of this session, which was longer and more powerful than the preceding three, Raymond looked at my mother for a long time. Then putting his face down close to hers he said, "Now you listen. I been here four times. Next time, you come to me. If you want to get strong, if you want to get rid of this thing [he pointed to the oxygen tank], if you want to get to *work*, then you know what you gotta do. You come to Sweat. Next Friday. Five o'clock."

My mother looked back at him in dismay. "But Raymond," she protested, "how can I? I'm not strong enough yet. That's why you've been coming here. You know I'm still very weak. Besides," she suddenly blurted, "that's Terry's fast date. She's planned her fast for that day. If I go up then, it will mean she'll have to postpone. I can't allow that."

Clearly, and uncharacteristically, she was afraid.

By that time I was standing at the foot of her bed. I suddenly heard myself say, "No! If you go, that will *be* my fast. If we really believe all the teachings of the past twelve years, all the wisdom and understanding, all the miracles we've seen, all the answered prayers, then we must do as Raymond says. You'll be protected. No harm will come to you. I stand before you to tell you I put my life on the line. Either we believe *truly* or we don't." I don't recall what else I said, but what

45

comes back to me, even now, is my sudden, powerful conviction that getting my mother to Sweat, by whatever means, was a directive from the Grandfathers that I could not ignore.

True, I had arranged to go into fast that weekend and had prepared for it for several days. But while I could postpone my fast, I didn't think my mother could put off this source of help much longer.

My mother looked long and hard at me, and I looked back. She knew I meant what I had said. "All right," she said, quietly. "I'll go."

"That's *good*," Raymond said. And it was settled.

Chapter Six

Not everyone shared my conviction. Iren was horrified when she was told the next morning. "If anything happens to your mother, Teruska, it will be all your fault. I will never forgive you."

It was an understandable reaction. Iren, and many of my mother's more secular friends, had never been to Sweat, nor could they possibly envision the extraordinary events that took place in those enclosed, sacred places. And even to those who were better informed it probably seemed very risky, perhaps irresponsible, to take an eighty-year-old person still dependent on an oxygen tank, with a badly damaged heart and a body only recently in remission from cancer, and expose her to the extreme heat of the rocks and the physical exertion of four "rounds" in a dark, airless lodge.

I had my own small spasms of doubt as the day approached, but by the time the designated Friday arrived, my mother's attitude had changed from anxiety to cheerful impatience. She could hardly wait to "get cracking," her favorite expression for taking on difficult but necessary tasks, and she urged us on as we rushed about getting ready to leave.

When it was time, when we had gathered all the food, sweat dresses, towels and my mother's own medicine tools, we gently lifted her from her bed, out the door, and into the Tioga. We placed the oxygen tank next to the makeshift bed after getting her comfortably tucked in.

I sat across from her and held fast to her hand while Edie, taking calm command at the wheel, drove off. The caretakers and some of the "regulars" followed behind. We wound slowly along, passing a herd of Tule Elk grazing near the Owens River, and caught sight of a Red-tail Hawk circling above the familiar convoy of ravens escorting us on our way.

We arrived in Big Pine shortly before five, to find Raymond waiting for us as we pulled into his yard and parked near the high wall that hides the Sweat Lodge from view. We could see smoke from the fire that had already been built to heat the large rocks collected earlier from a sacred place.

Three young men stood silently by. "These are my helpers," Raymond said, as they followed him into the Tioga. "They're gonna lift you up and take you in now." He smiled at my mother and softly patted the top of her head. "If you need them after, they'll help you back."

Wordlessly, they lifted her up and gingerly carried her ("like some mysterious sacred bundle," someone later described it) to the front of the Lodge. As they prepared to help her inside, suddenly Raymond told them they should let her go in on her own. "You get over to the west wall," he said. "You'll be all right now. I'll be right behind you."

We watched as my mother began to crawl on her knees and inch her way over the tule reeds, around the center pit to the open flap on the west side. It was a long and difficult progression and she was panting for breath when she reached the spot. Someone had placed the oxygen tank outside the wall, away from the dangers of the fire but within reach, if necessary. "She's not gonna need that tonight," Raymond said. "You better put it away."

With the utmost care he helped my mother stretch out on her back across the soft reeds, and when she seemed fairly comfortable he called to the rest of us to get ready to come in.

We quickly changed into our Sweat clothes and returned. Before entering we took up a handful of sage that had been laid out on the small mound, or altar, in front of the east entrance—the women first, the men following in the same manner. As we entered, Raymond indicated where he wanted us to sit. He motioned me over by my mother's feet.

After we were all in place, he called for the "doorman" to bring in the rocks. These were brought by pitchfork, two or three at a time, from the dwindling fire to the entrance.

From here, Raymond lifted them with a set of antlers he uses solely for this purpose. He carefully lowered them into the center pit; one by one, he

positioned the large, heavy and glowing volcanic
rocks which ~~represent the~~ core of our existence,
the Spirit Fire that breathes in all of us.

After all the rocks had been placed, blessed, and
sprinkled with certain herbs, a bucket containing
pure spring water that would generate the healing
steam was set in place. Raymond now asked the
doorman to close the entrance flaps. We sat in the
dark in that warm cocoon and waited for the
words that would signal the start of the first of my
mother's healing Sweats.

"Everybody ready?" Raymond asked, as he always does at this particular time. We answered in
a chorus of "yeses," "amens" and "hos." Above
our voices my mother said, "I'm ready, Raymond.
And I thank the Great Spirit for the help I will
receive."

"That's *good*," Raymond answered, and began
the familiar chant of the opening round.

As I sat among the others, listening to their
chants, joining my voice to theirs, my heart
cracked with love for my mother lying beside me,
gallantly surrendering to whatever the Grandfathers had in store. I thought of the hundreds of
times we had come here together over the years,
and the many more times she had been here on
her own, lending her strength to the people.
Strength, wisdom and understanding.

I remembered how carefully she had prepared
me for my first Sweat at a time when only a few
white faces could be seen among the regular at-
tendants. I recalled the surge of happiness I felt
and my sense of accomplishment when it was
over. She had told me what to expect and what to

50

do, but like many first experiences—falling in love, childbirth, separation, loss, recognition of a Higher Source—my imagination had fallen far short of the actual event.

The magic, the mystery of that first Sweat— seated next to my mother, giving our all to the Grandfathers, feeling her nudge me once or twice as if to say: What did I tell you? Isn't this *something*, the two of us here, sharing in such an ancient rite?—led to one of the more dramatic and decisive turning points in my life. Had it not been for this valiant trooper, this original, adventurous, spiritually-awake "little old lady," as she loved to call herself, I would have missed out on many of the marvels of the spiral journey.

"Bless yourselves," Raymond always says at the beginning and end of each round. "Pray for strength, wisdom and understanding."

The first round had come to a close. The flaps went up and a welcome breeze cooled our wet bodies. I noticed that breathing had become less difficult for my mother and that she could raise her head slightly to peer through the opening at the twilight sky. The flaps were ordered closed again and we went back to our labors—praying, chanting, blessing the healing heat and thanking the Spirit Helpers for coming in. "If you want something bad enough," Raymond often says, "You gotta *sweat* for it."

Between the third and fourth round my mother suddenly struggled to sit up.

"You lie down!" Raymond commanded. "Plenty of time to sit up later."

"Ah, Raymond," my mother sighed, in weak

51

Eve and Raymond Stone

protest. "You've finally got me where you want me. Flat on my back. In my place." That she could speak at all, let alone josh with Raymond about her place (a friendly bone of contention between them) was an early indication that our prayers had been heard. But the real proof—if, as often seems to be the case in our culture, we need visible confirmation—came when Sweat was over. When the last notes of the benediction chant had faded—the sweet slow song that honors the evening star as it crosses overhead, blessing us on its way—and we were getting ready to help my mother out, she announced firmly that this time she did not want to be carried, she wanted to walk. To walk!

"Ho!" said Raymond abruptly. "If she wants to walk, she'll walk. I'll stay with her. The rest of you go out. Get out of your hot pants [his term for our sweat clothes] and get ready to eat."

Reluctant to leave at first, we filed out one after the other into the cool night air. Exhausted and yet strangely exhilarated, we went to change our clothes. When we were dressed, we waited in an apprehensive cluster outside the community house for my mother and Raymond to emerge from the lodge.

After a long moment the two figures appeared, Raymond first and then my mother crawling out from the west opening. He helped her to her feet and called to me to bring a blanket. I ran to the Tioga, grabbed the first one I could find and brought it quickly to Raymond, who wrapped it around my mother's shoulders and her long wet dress. She stood between us, her face flushed from the Sweat, her short white hair matted down

53

against her head, a look of triumph in her eyes. Then, as everyone watched in undisguised amazement, she took her first wobbly yet determined steps. The distance between the Sweat Lodge and the community house where we traditionally gather after Sweat to sample the four ceremonial foods—Grandfather soup, bread, coffee and a thick berry filling called "gravy"—is only a few yards. But that evening it equaled the span of a marathon distance run. Step after measured step my mother moved toward the plain grey building until at last, to shouts of encouragement from Edie and the others, she reached the door.

"Shouldn't you rest now?" someone asked. "Shouldn't you lie down?"

"Yes I should," my mother answered, "but first I want to say the blessing."

"Well, what are we waiting for?" Raymond asked, as he beckoned everyone forward. "Let's eat!"

We flocked to the long pine tables inside and stood in silence while my mother bowed her head and said a short, moving prayer of thanks, ending with the familiar grace: "Bless this food to our use and bless the hands that prepared it. Bless our lives to Thy purpose." "Amen," we said in unison. As the others lined up to fill their plates, murmuring quietly among themselves, Raymond led my mother back to the Tioga. Edie and I followed closely behind. Raymond waited outside while we helped her change into dry clothes and eased her down onto the bed. With a long, contented sigh she settled in and closed her eyes. As if responding to a signal, Raymond climbed in and

54

sat beside her. He looked down at her for a second and then gestured to us to leave. We nodded that we understood. Squeezing through the back door and closing it softly behind us, we leaned against the cool frame of the Tioga and stared up at the brilliant night sky. Raymond joined us a few minutes later. "She's asleep," he told us. "You better go now. You drive careful. And watch how she does. She's gonna want to do things now. But you tell her she's gotta go slow. You come back next week. Same time." We thanked him with a hug and returned to the camper. Edie started the engine and we pulled away, saying little, each lost in our private thoughts. My mother slept peacefully as we drove through the valley. The mountains loomed on either side of us like dark, benevolent sentinels. The only signs of life along the way were rare flickers of light, from a car on a high curve, perhaps, or an isolated home.

As I peered out into the dark or glanced back at my mother from time to time, I wondered if she could hear my heart rattling in a crazy tattoo of pride and joy. I had my answer the next morning when I arrived to check on her. I found her sitting upright in her chair. She handed me an envelope and watched in affectionate curiosity as I opened it. Inside, on a card with a drawing of tiny oriental boats on a calm lake with a cherry tree in the foreground, she had written in a barely legible though familiar scrawl what turned out to be her last written communication to me. Among the thousands of letters we exchanged over the years, it remains the one I treasure most.

"Loved Terry," I read. "I can hardly wait to tell

you how much I love you and respect and admire your faith and fortitude. You restored mine which was badly wavering. You were wonderful throughout and especially yesterday. I lean on you so much. But now we have a flowering tree, two boats and space to go shining toward the promised land. Bless you and thank you. May all go to your heart's desire which is mine for you. Love from old Mum.''

Chapter Seven

In the days between the first of the healing Sweats in mid-June and the final one in early July, a series of small miracles took place. The most evident and immediate change was that my mother had no further need of the oxygen tank. She could now breathe on her own. The hated tubes, nose clips and other equipment were permanently banished from sight.

This, in turn, led to the next and most important event. To breathe freely meant taking up again what she had so deeply missed and had had to forego since February. She could—and would— smoke her Pipe again. Her decision to do so caused some initial alarm.

There were those who felt it could be physically harmful, and argued against it, begging her to reconsider. Regrettably, sharp words were exchanged. But in hindsight and on a human plane, they were an understandable and forgivable reaction to what had so recently happened and to my mother's steady transformation from dependent in-

valid to strong-willed spirit. She tolerated most of
the intrusions on her privacy and the liberties
taken with her "human envelope" for her general
good as part of the home care she received, but on
this matter she could not and would not be dis-
suaded. She overruled all objections.

Her Pipe, after all, was her most sacred possession. The integrity with which she smoked it had
never failed to bring about the healing blessing
that White Buffalo Woman has promised when her
gift to the people is "used aright." This was the
Pipe that had accompanied her through all her
years of service, through the trials and physical
setbacks, and through her many victories over pain
and suffering. This was the Pipe she had dedicated
herself to smoke on behalf of the world's "small
and large miseries" and had fasted specifically for
this power. This was the Pipe that gave birth to *I
Send a Voice*, in which she chronicled how it had
first come to her and the joyous path it subse-
quently led her on. This was the Pipe she had
shared with me on so many occasions "up the
hill," in a favored spot near a clear slow-running
stream, or in seclusion in her writing studio, or at
any place our paths happened to cross. This was
the Pipe she later introduced to my children and
the one that eventually led to my receiving one of
my own, carved from the same block of Pipestone
and by the same generous hands. This was the circle to which so many were drawn and from which,
in their turn, they were sent out to "go and help
the people."

So, on one clear night in June, accompanied by a
choir of crickets and the distant hooting of an owl,

58

my mother triumphantly prevailed. Edie and I sat on either side of her on the living room floor, and as the smoke from her Pipe drifted up and mingled with our own, all previous fears and doubts dissolved. The Grandfathers, as always, gave her the necessary protection and strength so that the ritual, rekindled after so long an interval, could be brought to its graceful conclusion with the words, or "affirmation" as my mother called it:

"And here we offer up ourselves with all that we are, all that we shall be as we soar shining. Uniting with the blessed company of all faithful creatures, all our relatives, throughout the worlds which You have made, and all those beings present, seen and unseen, we say yes, yes, yes, yes to Your Divine Will for us and for all that You have made."

This prayer, while drawn from several sources and longer versions, is so uniquely hers that to this day when others use it or I repeat it myself, her voice breaks through so distinctly and so clearly it's as though she were physically present and only inches away. A voice that Steven and Meredith Foster, founders of The School of Lost Borders, once described as "that subtle, lemon-sweet, cultured, motherly, wise, almost outrageous tone we will always associate with her teaching." It was not only her choice of the right words at the proper time, it was the educated English accent with which she delivered them that gave such an emphasis to what she had to say.

And credibility. Other factors lent credibility as well. Her long battle with cancer, and the many other aches and pains she endured with no trace

59

of self-pity, had brought her in closer touch with the men, women and children who came to her in failing health, in difficulty and in fear. She could talk to them with an authority born out of her own pain and send them off with the most potent of medicines, faith and hope.

"What we imagine, we can have." She was her own living proof. When the cancer had first struck she was given, at best, six months to live. With the help of healers—Raymond, Dr. G., and others, through the Kelly Institute and holistic approaches —she extended the sentence to eight years. But most of all, it was through her undivided faith in and religious use of her Pipe that she conquered the enemy within. Her unshakable faith in the power of prayer and the power of her Pipe, "uniting with the blessed company" lifted her high above the "surly bonds" and freed her for long intervals from the pull of her deteriorating cells.

After that initial night there were many more Pipes. Sometimes the caretakers took part, sometimes she smoked alone. Occasionally an unexpected guest arrived to "sit in the sacred manner" and share in this simplest of rites. On one particular evening—it may have been after the second of her healing Sweats—she lit her Pipe in the traditional way, offering tobacco to the four directions and as always, invited the Grandfathers to join in. When she had finished, she sat for a long time with her eyes closed and a wistful expression on her face. I sat beside her in relaxed silence. Suddenly she opened her eyes and cleared her throat. "Your father was here tonight," she announced. "He came and sat between us. He had many lov-

60

ing things to say to me. And to you. Did you feel
him here?''

"My *real* one?" I asked.

"Yes," she answered, smiling at the question.

If I have a gift for seeing things at certain times,
in certain places—an awareness of on-lookers and
"other-world" protectors—it is still at a fairly ele-
mentary level. I had not seen my father nor had I
felt his presence. I knew that my mother's father
was often an invited guest, but my own remained
as illusive a figure at this time as he had throughout my life. I didn't discover who he was until I
was nearly thirty. Until then I had always assumed
that the man my mother married in France—and
divorced very soon afterwards—was my father. A
citizen of Danzig, who, along with his entire family, would be murdered ten years later in a German concentration camp, not as a Jew, but as a
member of the "intelligentsia." Had my mother remained married to him, we would most certainly
have suffered the same fate. And no monument
(as is unfortunately still the case) would exist to re-
mind the world that in addition to six million Jews,
many millions more also perished in the holocaust.

It's not important how or when I came to learn
the facts of my real heritage. What *is* important is
that all through my childhood, though we were
often separated for long periods, my mother
always made me feel a most wanted and loved
product of her passionate love for my father. But
she was of an earlier, more discreet generation,
and had been badly hurt by a family who clung to
harsh Victorian mores and scorned the daughter
"wearing my apron high," as my mother wittily

described her unwed condition in her autobiography. My arrival caused such a furor that an irreconcilable rift developed between my mother and her own for many years. The shock to her family was not so much the unconventional and courageous decision to bear me alone as it was the family's fear of social embarrassment to my mother's sister, Lady Helen Dashwood. Yet one of the small ironies of their guarded, shoddy behavior was that my mother had met and fallen in love with my father at West Wycombe, my Aunt Helen's palatial English home.

At any rate my mother left for France to spare the family and, not incidentally, my father—a titled and married Englishman who held a high position at the University of London at the time. France is a country she had always loved, whose language she spoke fluently and among whose "citoyens" she now intended to live her life.

But even in France, to be a young, unmarried mother was not as generously accepted as one might expect of a country historically noted for courtly love. In my mother's day, the emphasis was more on court than courtly. To support us, to hold down a job, my mother needed papers. She needed the respectability of "Madame" before her name.

So when in sympathy with her plight, the young man from Danzig (a political refugee from his post as Professor of Economics at the University of Bonn) offered marriage, papers and an expedient divorce, she gratefully accepted.

She kept his name and citizenship for a number

of years. But when it became all too clear that Germany would once again try to dominate Europe, if not the world, and the chilling threat of war seemed certain, she left her beloved France and returned to England. While my mother found work in London and avoided the family, who now considered her status as a divorcee to be almost as scandalous as her original circumstances, I was enrolled in Wychwood School for Girls in Oxford, where, under the awesome tutelage of a Miss Pym, I gradually forgot my French and struggled to learn English.

Two years later, we were in Nova Scotia. Here, at last, her fortunes changed after the publication of her run-away best seller, *Quietly My Captain Waits*, and the sale of its movie rights. Life was never again as hard for her as it had been during the first two years of my existence. With no help from anyone, least of all my father, she still managed to provide a comfortable life for both of us.

Mine was a strange contrast between the rigid rules, stern religion and scratchy serge uniforms of the boarding school I attended nine months out of the year, and the wildly free summers my mother allowed me in Victoria Beach—a tiny fishing village on the coast of the Bay of Fundy. In my memory of this maritime province, land of the Micmacs and the Acadians, there is a blend of forty-foot tides, tall ships, small boats, shores lined with scallop shells, lobster traps and grey and white clapboard houses. There is a scent of pine trees, salt marshes, wild roses and crushed strawberries. There are the sounds of foghorns, seagulls, summer storms and an Irish brogue in the voices of the fishermen trading stories around pot-bellied stoves.

There is no picture of my father here. Only my mother, hard at work in her studio in Fundy Tide —the home she designed and loved above all others—and the apple trees I sat beneath, the cliffs I clambered down, the woods I intrepedly explored, the barns I took refuge in, and the winding village road I loped along.

I was glad my father had come to sit with us that night. His visit seemed a long-awaited and significant completion of an important cycle. "All our relatives," we say before we enter Sweat or smoke our Pipes. Since that evening I now specifically invite my father to join me. On rare occasions I sense his presence and feel him watching me with interest and perhaps with genuine concern for my current well-being.

Sometimes they come together, my mother and my father. When they do, I mentally hop over to greet them like a crow whose wings have been clipped but who knows that they will mend, who knows that when she dares to fly again, she will still be able to race with the wind.

Chapter Eight

During these days of steady progress, additional healing Sweats, continued Pipe ceremonies and the general consensus that a critical corner had been turned, other, and thankfully more visible, relatives appeared. The first among these, in late June, was my daughter Marty, with three-year-old Meghan in tow—my mother's great-granddaughter, whom she had not yet met. This visit, like the others to follow, was anticipated with much joy. Careful plans were laid for the few days they would be in Independence. Much thought was given to dress, to the selection of appropriate gifts and to the apportioning of time so that there would be plenty of rest periods to preserve my mother's strength for this special occasion.

There had always been a singularly close, affectionate bond between my mother and her grandchildren, the "non-adopted ones," as David possessively pointed out in one of his letters. It began at birth and remained a consistent thread throughout their childhood and into their young adult years. She had always been the anchor and the trusted keeper of their secrets. From an early age they knew her as the dispenser of special treats and imaginative presents whenever she visited us at our various addresses. We moved so often— from New York to Virginia, Iowa, Nebraska, Minnesota and Indiana—that she claimed to need a map with multicolored pins just to keep track. But she always found us and settled in for a few days at a time, surrounded by the children and a continual menagerie under our roof, which at one interval included a small alligator. After she moved to California her visits were less frequent, but they are indelibly remembered as periods of abundant fun, innocent mischief, magic and fairy tales and, as her own path gradually developed in this direction, as their introduction to the Grandfathers.

I have mentioned the alligator. In her early delvings into American Indian traditions, my mother took part in a "blessing of the animals" ceremony and called to tell me about it a few days later. We were living in Iowa then, in a wonderful rambling old house with a long back porch and large yard, into which, during a short-lived period, an elderly dog, a litter of kittens, a small barn owl and a moth-eaten possum had mysteriously found their way. The alligator made its appearance also, but from another direction. Some prankster had put it in Marty's locker at school and, quite naturally, she had brought it home. Much to the children's delight and my rapidly waning enthusiasm, we had managed to add this strange assortment to our own resident dog, cat, hamster and mouse.

As soon as my mother called to describe her part

in the ceremony, I understood. I told her what had been happening. "Please darling," I implored, "the next time you're invited to bless the animals, could you possibly reduce your enthusiasm by about half?" My mother laughed and laughed. She said she must have somehow turned herself into an "Aunt Clara," that well-meaning and befuddled TV sorceress on "Bewitched," whose spells consistently missed their mark with chaotic results. My children never doubted their grandmother's gift for magic, nor did it ever matter to them if it sometimes went slightly awry. They simply accepted the fact that they had a unique and unusual Gran and felt sorry for those who didn't.

Not many of their friends, after all, had a grandmother who wrote books that could be found in every library, on every imaginable subject from Isis to Hung Tu, from Edward III to Pasco Paoli, from Acadians to Cajuns, from humorous vignettes for *The New Yorker* to spiritual works for the New Age.

Nor did they know of many grandmothers who had flown around the world as a war correspondent and now drove fearlessly across the continent, alone, accepting each adventure and setback as a gift from Those Above to be met with humor, and a willing heart. Nor did other grandmothers seem to arrive with a suitcase full of "roughies," a collection of small rocks she had glued together to form unusual little people and animals—treasures that had been especially blessed for their new owners and stood guard on their shelves.

A lonely and unhappy childhood had kept her in tune with the vulnerability of children. The cardinal sin, in her view, was to dash their hopes,

67

make cruel fun, or hurt a child's feelings. "God is not a Dampe," she would say, quoting John Donne, "so I shouldn't be one either." And proved the point through kind laughter and an un-flinching support for the four budding timpanists, trumpeters, shy poets and playwrights for whom she was often a captive audience.

On the rare occasions that sibling arguments erupted in her presence, it was she who intro-duced the burning of sage to clear away the sulks or bad atmosphere, and taught that "medicine" is not a bad-tasting tonic but means how we spend our days, each in itself a perfect gift, and how we enrich ourselves and others by commitment to the work we choose. And again, proved it by example.

For my mother's eightieth birthday, Marty wrote a long and loving tribute in which she said, in part:

"You are the only person about whom I can say I have only happy memories. I can't remember, can't even imagine an unhappy or unpleasant time with you. There are a lot of scenes from when I was very small...after you came to Sweet Briar and built Pangur it was wonderful to know that we could see you often. [Marty's father was an English professor at Randolph Macon Women's College in Lynchburg, Virginia, and we lived only a few miles from Sweet Briar at the time.]

"I remember Pangur as if I left it yesterday: how it looked, how it smelled, how the straw rug felt on my feet. I remember your silk sheets and an amber necklace you showed me once, and a piece of polished amethyst you gave me, and a little wooden chest filled with coins you gave me for my

birthday. [Marty was five.] There was the red-
handled silverware, and the incense you burned in
the writing room, and your father's sword by the
door, and the pot-bellied stove.

"I remember swimming in the lake and sitting
on the lawn afterwards. My first and only taste of
caviar was at your house! I remember staying overnight once or twice and listening to Iren play the
piano as I went to sleep. It was all pure happiness.
It can't be just a child's tendency to see everything
as good; just being with you made me happy (and
still does). How can you doubt that people love
you?

"Then you left Sweet Briar and went to Ohio
and then to California. We moved to Fairfield
[Iowa] and everything was very disconnected for a
while, until we came to Lone Pine to visit you. I
loved your house by the stream and the chickens. I
still feel very 'connected' to that part of the world
even though your house is no longer there. [This
was the small cabin that was bulldozed away by
the Bureau of Land Management, which caused
the cancellation of all future concerts in the Alabama Hills.] I love the desert and the empty spaces
. . . .I love being out where you could hear the
emptiness.

"The last 20 years. . .we haven't had much time
together physically but I think the spiritual connection has grown even stronger. I feel I have inherited some of your gifts, even though I don't have
'the will to believe' which has taken you so far in
the Indian way. I believe that this way of finding
the center makes more sense than any other. . .
every place has its own gods; every person has her

own way of finding them....Having you as part of my life has made all the difference. I wasn't kidding when I told my friends I didn't have any worries when I was expecting the kids [She named her first after my mother's father, Daniel Vernon, which made my mother very happy] because I knew my grandmother was watching over me. I know that when you go to the next life you will still watch over all of us and still be with us as you have always been. But after being with you for 32 years I cannot imagine life without you in it.

"I'm not particularly good at expressing the 'positive' emotions—eloquent though I may be when I get mad!—and I know you sometimes have trouble believing that people love you and value you. But between us there has always been a special bond though neither of us may be able to put it in words, if indeed we really need to. I just wanted to try somehow to put my side of it on paper for you. I want to thank you for all the happiness you've brought into my life and make some feeble attempt to put my love into words...."

On the long-awaited arrival day, I went to Las Vegas to meet Marty and Meghan's plane. One of the disadvantages (though some might think it an advantage) of living in Owens Valley is the impossibility of direct flights for anyone coming from long distances. Marty chose Las Vegas over Los Angeles for economic reasons, and I wasn't unhappy with the choice.

The drive is long but it covers spectacular territory. I love to drive, letting my thoughts hum along in rhythm with the wheels on the road. I inherited this trait from my mother. From the moment she purchased her first car—a Baby Austen put together with bailing wire, followed in more affluent days by a succession of Mercury convertibles, one of the first four-wheel-drive International Harvester Scouts, a Volkswagen "Beetle" and, at the last, a Datsun pickup with a camper shell—she took off at the slightest excuse, like Toad of Toad Hall in the *Wind in the Willows*. Nothing gave her more pleasure than to "tool around" the countryside and explore back roads and hidden valleys. Once, at MacDowell Colony in Peterborough, New Hampshire, she inherited a 1928 Plymouth roadster which she named "Phidipedes" and drove as lightheartedly as she might have driven a Rolls-Royce, in spite of having to restrict her "spins" to daytime since the headlights worked on separate batteries that continually died out.

One of the most difficult adjustments she had had to make in her later years was to have someone else at the wheel. Whenever she could get away with it she would sneak off in her pickup and drive to favorite spots in the valley or up in the mountains, and return with a very pleased expression and a very deaf ear to all the protests that predictably followed. Had she been able to, she would most certainly have accompanied me on this trip to pick up Marty and Meghan.

They were waiting for me amid the clatter of coins falling from one-armed bandits at the airport. We spent the night in a nearby motel, overjoyed to be in one another's company again. Although this was Meghan's first flight and her first venture away from Kansas, she adapted like the regular member of the Eaton clan she gives every indication of being. A grandma's bias, I suppose, but I do detect signs....

We made an early start the next morning (difficult for Marty who shares our night-owl tendencies) and drove merrily back, climbing steadily toward the Inyo-White Mountain range on the tortuous, roller-coaster road that cuts through Westgaard Pass. As we maneuvered the hairpin curves, we drove past Deep Springs College—that extraordinary, isolated "working ranch" campus, where for two years my mother had been the entire English *and* French departments to a student body of twenty select young men.

She had loved the place. She describes her brief tenure there in the most lyrical of terms in *The Trees and Fields Went the Other Way*. The students were bright and receptive, and she spent long and fruitful hours with them, sometimes in a classroom but mainly on horseback or in her four-wheel-drive helping to round up cattle (part of the curriculum). And somewhere along the way, she introduced them to Boswell and Pasquale Paoli, Dante and Keats, Molière and Jane Austen, either high among Juniper trees, or—in a sacred place further north—beneath Bristlecone pines, the oldest living trees on earth.

I told Marty of the stormy night I had sat next to Raymond in his truck while Evalina and my mother rode behind, covering this same road to Deep Springs so that Raymond could donate a figure he had carved out of pipestone—a warrior holding a Pipe in his outstretched hands—in honor of a student who had been killed in Vietnam. It was Raymond's give-away, his thanks for the safe

72

return of his own sons from that far-off war in a
faraway land. It is still there, in a place of honor in
the library—keeping watch, I like to think, over my
mother's many books on the shelves.

Hot, tired and hungry, we arrived at the house
in Independence in late afternoon. We were
greeted by a welcoming committee of Edie, Iren
and my mother, who had selected a long bright
shift and a large yellow medallion to wear for this
momentous occasion—her introduction to Meghan.
They approved of each other on sight. After shyly
sizing one another up, they broke into smiles of
recognition, an instant acknowledgement of the
"important personage" each would surely become
to the other.

Meghan let go of Marty's hand and skipped toward her great-grandmother, who was sitting in an
overstuffed chair next to a wall covered with gaily
colored streamers, cards and balloons. She placed
her small hands on my mother's knees and guile-
lessly looked up at her elder. "Hi Gran," she
chirped. "I like it here. I like you." My mother
beamed back in delight and pointed to a package
she had been holding. "Here Meghan," she said.
"This is for you. Open it and see what it is."

Meghan slowly pulled off the wrapping paper
and ribbon, and refusing all offers of help, she
lifted out a handmade Teddy Bear. "He told me
you were coming," my mother said, "and that he
wants to live with you. What do you think you'll
call him?" Meghan looked at the bear for a minute
and then she solemnly said, "His name is Meghan's Bear." That settled, she did a tiny pirouette
and went hopping back to her mother.

It was not long after this exchange that my
mother wrote the following commemorative poem,
which with one other turned out to be the last two
poems and the last words she would write in this
lifetime.

> Meghan came round the white leg
>   of the table.
> Three-year-old Meghan, right size
>   for delights.
> Bear was waiting for her on great-
>   grandmother's lap
> More than half alive. Power animal
> Somewhere between an angel and a
>   toy
> Made by friendly hands
> and stuffed full with delights
>   for Meghan.
> Good medicine for Meghan.
> The meeting was conclusive
> Bear arms went out,
> white arms enfolded.
> "What will you call him?" Great-
>   Grandmother asked.
> "His name is Meghan's Bear," she
>   said. "Meghan's Bear."

Watching Meghan's open delight in her new
possession, I saw myself at a slightly older age,
clutching a bear with similar features and stuffed
with the same "good medicine." I was six years
old and we were, for some obscure reason, in
Hastings, England, the site of William the Con-
queror's victorious battle in 1066. But it was then

74

1936 and must have been soon after our arrival from France, as I still spoke only French.

I remember a garden and I remember a bee. And the startling pain of my first bee sting. I was outraged. "Why?" I demanded to know. "Why would it want to hurt me?"

"It's because you look so sweet it thought you were a flower, and when you tried to brush it off it got upset and frightened because flowers don't usually do that. Besides, it's an *English* bee. It doesn't understand French."

"I don't like English bees," I pouted.

"No, of course not. I don't either. French ones have much better manners."

I know the sequence of this conversation well because my mother repeated it many times, explaining how badly she'd felt that our pleasant outing had been so rudely shattered. What could she do to mollify the sniffling, anxious child at her side, who was probably already unsettled by this move to a foreign land and by leaving behind all that she had loved and understood in France.

She bought me a bear. A honey-colored bear who was, she told me, very sorry that I had been stung by a bee and who wanted to make up for it. She explained that bears know all about bees because they like honey and that they sometimes get stung too, when they attempt to steal some from a bee's house. She told me I should try to forgive the bee because stinging is its only means of defense and once it does that it stops living. A bee's having to die in order to cause me such pain was an altogether new concept for me. It seemed a very steep price to pay.

I named the bear "Teds" and took him every-where. He was my confidant in whispered conver-sation late at night, in the spartan cubicle that was my refuge at Edgehill Church School for Girls, a transplanted English boarding school in Windsor, Nova Scotia, whose rules and regulations I sur-vived for seven years and left, at age fifteen, battle-scarred but undaunted, and vigorously equipped to take on almost anything else in life. Teds travelled with me to America, to Walnut Hill, a preparatory school in Natick, Massachusetts, where I spent a year in culture shock, in unac-customed freedom and in lively pursuit of prep school boys, those mysterious creatures we had been forbidden to think of or speak about at Edgehill.

The bear survived my college years at Briarcliff in New York, and my summers in Quaker Hill as well as my apprenticeship at The Starlight Theatre, a summer stock company my mother enthusiasti-cally encouraged me to join and whose expensive fee she generously paid. Later, when I moved into an apartment in New York City—where I was an aspiring actress whiling the days away in a gloomy office at *McCall's Magazine*, waiting for my "break" —the bear came too. And when I married Dick Brengle and settled in with him at Shanks Vil-lage—a reconverted army camp whose barracks were now home for ex-G.I.s attending Columbia University—we found a place for Teds. On her fre-quent visits to the first, if makeshift home of my married life, my mother was amused to find this link to my childhood on the pillow of our bed. And a year later, he was at the foot of Marty's crib, which we had tucked into a corner of the pantry and transformed into a nursery.

Like Meghan's, this was no ordinary bear. Had it not been for his untimely end at the venerable age of twenty-two, when one of the children accidentally lost him in the brush behind our house in Lynchburg, Virginia, (where we later found him de-stuffed and decomposed) he would certainly be here with me in San Diego. Or, more likely, in Glendale two hours away, where Meghan now lives with her parents and her brother Dan, to sit on a shelf with "Meghan's Bear."

Chapter Nine

In my mother's garden—a mosaic of flowers amid lilac bushes and bountiful fruit trees—a statue of Saint Francis with pronounced American Indian features, which Raymond had carved from pipestone, stood guard in a tall bird bath filled with specially chosen rocks. Near this, but hidden from view by a tightly woven screen of willow branches and a lattice of climbing roses, was a large round horse trough made of corrugated metal and filled with ice-cold water on summer days.

This was the "Guru bath" my mother had retrieved from a local dump to set up in this spot, which was perfect for cooling herself after long hours at the typewriter. Or, more accurately, for cleansing away any accumulated doubts or "negativities." For as long as I can remember my mother had found ways to live or be near water sources, or, if that was impossible, to find a tub, a shower, or even a garden hose to use for spiritual purposes. From the Mediterranean to the Bay of Fundy—or a pond fed by rust-colored streams at "Two Brooks" (her home in Quaker Hill), a creek in Lone Pine that was "turned on and off" at the whim of the Department of Water and Power, or the horse trough in Independence—she spent a part of each day plunged in cold water as a private act of purification, an ablution.

Sometimes the water was extremely hot. One of her more satisfying discoveries when she first moved to the Owens Valley was the Keogh Hot Springs just north of Big Pine, in the foothills of the Sierra. For as long as she could, she went alone, or in a group, to soak in the steaming mineral waters of that ancient meandering stream that draws its source from beneath the earth's crust. The hot springs attracts a variety of people, usually weekend skiers en route to Mammoth or other travellers, local residents and a few who understand its healing properties and have learned to respect the tradition of quietly waiting one's turn and of keeping the surrounding area as free of debris as possible.

On occasion, if my mother found a "bunch of rowdies" at her favorite pools along the stream, she would patiently wait for them to emerge, dry themselves, and then she would "brief" them in no uncertain terms on the proper approach to the springs, and the need to remember one's manners at such a sacred place. She would introduce herself as the official "scold," and whether or not they remembered to leave loud radios and alcohol behind on future visits, they were certainly startled into silence and a hasty retreat on this one. And she was right. To lie back in those hot waters late at night, under a canopy of stars, is to commune with the Great Mysterious in a way that is incom-

79

parable to any other. On winter nights we had the thermal baths and on hot June afternoons when temperatures commonly climb to 103 degrees and higher, the "Guru bath" was a welcome reprieve.

During Marty and Meghan's stay we paced their visits so as to not overtire my mother. We divided our time among playing "pooh sticks" from a small wooden bridge that crossed the stream near my trailer, exploring gravel paths that led to groves and to wide-open spaces broken only by sagebrush and giant, perfect-for-climbing boulders, walking to the fish hatchery to feed the rainbow trout in the crystal-clear lake and driving down to call on great-grandmother.

Two days after her arrival, Meghan discovered the "guru bath." Off went her clothes. Off went mine. And in we plunged, laughing and dunking up and down in unvarnished pleasure. Soon Marty joined in, and then Edie—each of us taking turns lifting Meghan in and out.

We had thought my mother asleep while we romped, but she had heard our shrieks and happy shouts, and had insisted that she be helped down the steps and along the path lined with hollyhocks that led from Edie's house to her own. She inched her way to the willow screen and peered through it unobserved until Meghan spotted her a few moments later.

"Great-gran!" she whooped. "What are *you* doing here?"

"Watching you, Meghan, that's what. I haven't seen such a lovely sight for centuries."

Meghan scrambled out, wriggled happily as

Terry and Meghan at the ''Guru bath''

Four generations—Eve, Marty, Meghan, Terry

Marty dried her, and broke loose to run to her great-grandmother.

It was this gay and innocent event that sparked the second and final poem my mother wrote:

> Meghan came to the horse trough
> (We call it the Guru bath, the
>   Meditation pool)
> On a hot day.
> Behind the trellis of willow twigs
> Beneath the roof of roses
> She stood encountering coolness
> From the snows, the run-off,
> The top of Onion Valley, the
> Top of Oak Creek.
> There were cries and splashings. An
> Elder held her safe.
> "Grandma helped me out," she
> Cried and ran to tell great-grandma
> the event. Mother towelled her
> And took her on her lap.
> Four generations of women
> Happy in the joy of the three-
>   Year-old's water embrace.
>
> Simple joys—simple joys!

Shortly after Meghan's "water embrace," someone, thankfully, had the foresight to take a polaroid picture of the four of us together. My mother is seated in a garden chair, in her long green-patterned dress and a pair of fuzzy bedroom slippers. Marty and I are clustered around her, and Meghan, wrapped in a towel, is perched on Marty's lap. Seconds before the shutter clicked, my mother had placed her sun hat on top of my head, and there we are, the four generations, "contemporaries with different sets of memories," smiling out at the world in a captured memory of that charmed afternoon.

I did not see then, as I do now whenever I look at this photo, how very frail my mother was, nor did I fully appreciate, in the set of her jaw, how much courage and determination it had taken for her to rise to this occasion and take part in the "simple joy." This too was an ingrained part of her creed. To put on one's best bib and tucker, to "take the elevator" when an exceptional occasion called for it. She neither understood nor endorsed the self-indulgences, the old "let it all hang out" attitude that marked the behavior of some of the younger generation and, she noted with disappointment, some of the older ones too.

My mother's approach to the way of things was simple, direct and devoid of ego. One should move with one's best face, one's best foot forward, despite private pain, fatigue or frustrating setbacks. Move at a steady pace, in the turtle steps an elder had described to her as the "go slow way," the "no feel way." Walk gently and listen to the breathing underneath the feet. "Puttin' off the agony, puttin' on the style," as the song goes.

It was a style that still sets her apart from most people and one that certain of today's so-called spiritual leaders, healers and even Shamaness as one woman currently in vogue calls herself, might do well to study and practice. Unlike some of the more acquisitive guides, my mother never charged

exorbitant fees for her talks. Nor did she ever offer
what she called "fast-food" medicine with prom-
ises of instant shamanism or of instant anything-
ism to those willing to pay the price. And miss
out, in their hurry, on the discipline and the fun to
be had in slow discoveries, and the genuinely simple joys.

Another picture that comes to mind when I look
at the four generations is one that was taken at
Marty's wedding in 1972. My mother and the minister are standing back to back, each with arms up
in supplication or in blessing, and my mother is
facing the bride and groom while the minister is
turned away from them. Yet when this picture was
snapped, the minister was actually standing direct-
ly in front of Marty and Jim, and my mother was
off to the side among the small collection of
parents and friends who had come long ways to
"gather in the presence" of this young couple who
had chosen to exchange vows near an ancient burial ground in the middle of a Wisconsin State Park.

Commonplace today, but then it was known as a
"happening," a rejection of the traditional and a
strike for independence. As the invited guests to
this particular "happening," we formed a group of
slightly bewildered onlookers. Unsure of protocol
but anxious to please, we were determined to
show our support for the young couple. Jim's parents—conservative Republicans from upstate New
York—faced a greater challenge perhaps than we,
as Marty's parents did, since we had spent most of
our married lives on one campus or another and
were presumably more in tune with the spirit of
the sixties and seventies. Still, while swatting off

swarms of mosquitos and shuffling about among
the trees, in a somewhat disorganized circle, even
we couldn't help thinking rather wistfully of the
small Episcopalian church and the large Victorian
house where we had earlier thought this great
event might take place.

In my mother's journal entry for September 24
she wrote:

"A little procession of cars with uncertain people—except for the first car leading the way with
bride and groom. Uncertain? Yes, because they
would not have done it this way, would not see it
done as they would have liked, because they loved
their young folk, the son, the daughter and had
dreams for them—and now were set aside and all
their values negated—and yet relied on in some
anxious way, to be there, to approve, to make an
effort—a great effort—to support these young people in their parade of conventional unconven-
tionality.

"So, elderly aunts on Jim's side donned slacks,
some obviously for the first time and only time,
and others wore new sports clothes. The two families eyed each other speculatively, sympathetically,
anxiously and were reassured. They were all wearing the appropriate thing, a little self-consciously,
or a little regretfully, for it would have been good
to wear a pretty dress or see others in pretty
dresses. But this was the young folks' day—and
way—and there was genuine love and tenderness
for them. The young folk too had made an effort
in dress.

"The blue jeans were changed for a better looking pair and the bridegroom's shirt was new,

85

made by the bride, with special pearl buttons and puffed sleeves. He had discarded his head band, his hair was shining clean and he wore the little arrowhead the grandmother of the bride had brought him. The bride had made her dress, apple green, long, pretty. She carried no flowers, wore no ornaments.

"All got out of the cars and walked toward the select place, a shady corner of the park, beneath trees.

"And the ceremony, studiously casual, began.

" 'We have gathered to recognize a relationship that has grown between this woman and this man...' "—words to that effect. A clear message that the wedding is not now, that the marriage is a fact we are, perhaps tardily, there to recognize. No, not tardily. This was the right moment for the recognition. The young people chose it, September 24. It is obvious that there is importance to them in all that they do and don't do at this wedding.

"No music, no lights. No bridesmaids. No best man. The bride's small brother has a part, however. He holds the rings and produces them at the right time.

"The bridal couple say alternate speeches to each other about marriage. The bride's grandmother gives a Paiute message:

" 'I am empowered by the Paiutes of Owens Valley to give these young people a message. The Grandfathers say: Stand tall and proud. May you sing the same song as you walk together toward the blessing of the Great Spirit. May your marriage bring happiness to you, to those who love you, to those whom you love. Hyeh, hyeh, hyeh.'

"The minister reads the Gospel of St. John. He

says 'let us pray,' a short prayer for blessing upon the two who now give each other a prolonged and hearty kiss. And that's it. It is over. No giving the woman. No pronouncing man and wife. No fuss, no flapdoodle.

"A very real and moving wedding, made so not only by the planning of the young folk but by the love and flexibility and sacrifices of both families who have come so far for the ceremony. The carefully unceremonious ceremony, adhering to the principle that people should have their weddings the way that *they* want to have them.

"The father of the bride felt a little like the forgotten man. The mother of the bride was more 'with it' but was a little worried in anticipation of the reception which the newlyweds wanted in their own apartment, the one they had already shared for several months in an open secret but neither set of parents knew if the other "knew" ...and when she saw the bride in her wedding dress washing cups and saucers at the primitive little sink, and a large pile of garbage no one had remembered to take out, and the somewhat pitiful little presents, again by request, and yet—looking at the faces and the firm fondness of all the sophisticated, worldly, well-off, some of them very rich—people going through their paces round the garbage pile—there was so much good will and real tolerance, understanding, fondness, that these two, so independent yet so pleased to be supported in what they were doing—must surely be off to a good start—as good a start as any marriage has.

"One felt so. One felt the reactions of all these people. Uncle Barry from his huge, streamlined job, his New York life, handing us in and out of the family V. W. bus, the wedding bus, and always ready to pick up the tab. Uncle Tom, on the bridegroom's side, taking swift nips and disappearing frequently to do so—yet always the suave, good-humored man-of-the-world gentleman...with two such uncles surely the pair are off to a great worldly start.

"Many aunts appraising the bride's mother with genuine liking and sympathy for what every woman knew she must be feeling. After all, one wants something a little...a little... 'I don't suppose this is *just* what she imagined for her daughter's wedding?'

" 'No. But it's what the young folks wanted and insisted on...so fine. Fine.'

"The children running about stuffing themselves on the heart-shaped cookies the bride had made. No wedding cake, no champagne. A new style wedding, in the national park of their college town.

"The bride's parents have a lovely home and would have liked—did suggest—a simple wedding here with the family minister, Jim Fallis, their good friend. The generation that proclaims it is never listened to, never heard, was as usual deferred to— with love—and complete support. Now it is up to them."

Of us all, it was my mother who had travelled the longest distance, driving from California to give her personal support and to deliver the unexpected Paiute blessing which, while somewhat startling at the time, is now remembered as the highlight of the ceremony.

On her return, she stopped at Pipestone, Minnesota, to select a large and heavy slab of catlinite to bring back to Raymond. It was from this smooth red rock that Raymond later carved my mother's Pipe, many of his "whittling" figures and, later, a small Pipe for me which Evalina calls my "night Pipe" since it has the outline of a new moon and what appears to be a galaxy of stars on either side of the bowl.

My mother was later asked to conduct many more weddings, large and small, but I doubt that any gave her more pleasure than that particular one. Unless it had been John's, my eldest son's, which unhappily for all concerned she wasn't able to attend.

She sent loving messages and noted with amusement that the pendulum had swung in the opposite direction. In 1982, John and Nancy opted for *their* new way, a large church wedding under bowers of flowers, accompanied by a young, nervous harpist, and conducted by a Presbyterian minister and our old Episcopalian friend Jim, elevated now to Archbishop, who kept the occasion from becoming too solemn by losing his place in the Holy Matrimony service several times.

At the outdoor reception, while guests milled about, spilling punch and anxiously eyeing the clouds that threatened rain, I scanned the skies for other signs and saw them clearly. Three large crows flew overhead, circled above us and disappeared. "Three crows a wedding," I said to John and he smiled and answered, "I think I know who sent them."

89

Chapter Ten

Marty and Meghan had arrived shortly after the second of my mother's healing Sweats, and they flew back to Kansas just prior to the third, leaving us much to think about, to laugh over, and prompting my mother's brief, creative spurt which resulted in the two poems.

The Sweats were obviously helping, not only in reviving my mother's spirits but in extending the periods of time for which she felt able to be up and about. Her "overcoat" was very worn, but the underpinnings shone through like the beam of a lighthouse from an opposite shore.

In a burst of energy, my mother now began to talk at length about a plan she had been mulling over for some time. It had first come to her in a dream and then later as a prediction from someone she had met at Dr. G.'s in San Jose during one of her many trips there as a patient and close friend.

Her vision, which she talked about with a real sense of urgency, was that she should somehow be the instrument through which a council could be held—a gathering of many Medicine Men or chiefs, who would come together in strength and harmony to work for the common good.

The prediction, as related in her journal in 1979, read:

"Joyce told me today a lot about crystals. She told us to sleep with our crystals under the pillow tonight. I finally asked her what she saw about me. Two years ago, in London, out of the blue she had told me she saw me 'teaching young white people the Indian way' which at the time seemed to me unlikely, yet two years later that was exactly what I was doing. Now she sees me in 'politics' which has always seemed to me the no-no of no-nos. She sees me with foreign politicians 'speaking my language'—the only one I have is French—getting support and funding for a meeting of many great Indian Chiefs and Shamans—at odds with themselves—(they are!) and I arrange a meeting of these Indian leaders, promising them seclusion and secrecy. I provide the food and protection. They come separately, not knowing who will be there. I have gone to them separately and arranged it all—(perhaps through Draco?). Then she sees that I do not sit down with them, nor any woman (very likely—typical in fact)—but they have learned to trust me. One factor is my age. And she sees the meeting as a 'last stand.' If they can't agree to work together that will be that. She sees the meeting a success. And afterward I am rewarded with a very sacred honor for having arranged it. Well, of course, lately I have been building bridges, I do know some of them and I have leads to more."

When she had been at Esalen the final time, she had tentatively discussed the possibility of holding

91

the meeting there, and the idea was being considered. Also, she had been sent word by another leader that she should go first to England then, in 1983, France and Germany to speak to certain groups and request donations for something that would be made clear to her when the time was right. Or, the leader told her, if she couldn't go she must send an ambassador of good will in her place.

She spoke to us of this now, and insisted we get word to the three or four Medicine Men she thought would be receptive and most likely to share in the plan. They, in turn, would inform others and the proposed council would grow and spread. Only Raymond responded. The others, giving vague and evasive excuses, declined the invitation. When we reported this, she was deeply disappointed but nevertheless resigned.

Most of her ideas, visionary or otherwise, were generally ten years ahead of the times, a fact which had often handicapped the sale of some of her books. They appeared typically long before the general populace was ready for them. *Flight*—a metaphysical, modern-day *Pilgrim's Progress* or *Everyman*, and her particular favorite—was published in 1954, the decade of spiritual apathy and political witch-hunts. *Go Ask the River*—her lilting, carefully researched story of Hung Tu, the eighth-century Chinese poetess—came out in 1969 when relations with China were at their worst and not due to improve until the seventies.

The King Is a Witch, a compelling account of the Old Religion, or witchcraft, as practiced by King Edward III, was published in 1965, many years

92

ahead of the current, renewed interest in the "pagan" ways. And even *Snowy Earth Comes Gliding* was rejected by so many publishers that she decided to print it privately. Later, through an enduring, affectionate bond and the mutual respect of one writer for another, as well as for the subject matter, Wabun James got it published through Bear Tribe Publications. Fortunately it is still in print and getting the attention it deserves.

"It must be so frustrating to always be so far ahead of the rest of us," I told her in sympathy when I saw how dejected and close to tears she had become at this latest rebuff. "But I'm certain your dream will come about, as almost all your other ones have, sooner or later."

"It's their choice," she sighed. "I've done my part. Now it's up to them. Let me see....By my usual miscalculations, they should be starting to think about thinking about the idea in 1993." She seldom referred to the proposed council again.

Ironically, one "no-no" part of the prediction did come about in late September of 1981. My mother was asked to take part in a peaceful gathering at Diablo Canyon near San Luis Obispo, to seek protection for the area surrounding the much-in-dispute nuclear energy plant and a blessing for Mother Earth. There had been many demonstrations at the site previously, resulting in the usual arrests and upheavals, but this coming together— sponsored by Heymeyohsts Storm and Harley Swift Deer, two leaders of an organization called Metis, to which my mother had been designated the official "Grandmother"—was planned as a nonviolent operation.

Peaceful demonstration at Diablo Canyon. Surft Turtle, Eve, and PG&E Nuclear Energy representative

My mother had met Heymeyohsts at U. C. Berkeley, during a symposium presented by the St. George Homes, or New Age Residential Treatment Center for Schizophrenic and Autistic Adolescents, and based loosely on Storm's beautiful and classic book, *Seven Arrows*. She greatly admired his work and many of the things Storm stood for, and although she was troubled by some of his practices, she remained genuinely fond of "Peck's Bad Boy," as she dubbed him.

It was Storm who, later in the year (November, 1981), would erect and consecrate a small Rainbow-Kachina Lodge for my mother's use and at the same time, "by the power vested" in him, name her a Medicine Woman and healer. Two generous friends, Myron and Jean Stolaroff, graciously agreed to have it built on their property in the Indian Hills area of Lone Pine, in a secluded spot sheltered by ancient giant boulders near an inviting pond.

This was during a period in which Raymond had been pressured by both his own people and outside forces to deny non-Indians as much access to his Lodge as before. We were suddenly segregated to Sweats for non-Indians only, once a month—the other three weeks to be exclusively for Indians. As it had always been a singular privilege to attend at all, we were hardly in a position to object. But there were hurt feelings and disappointments during this short-lived episode.

A Navajo man was particularly upset because, as he told us, he never felt very welcome in the Paiute community and preferred to sweat with his

95

white friends. A Filipino woman didn't know where she fit and ended up going to both groups.

Eventually, Raymond reversed himself and renewed his vow to accept any and all who came and sincerely asked, or needed healing, but until this change of heart, it was especially inconvenient for my mother, so to have her own small Lodge was, in her words, "magic and overwhelming." It was indeed a place of magic for, among other blessings, rainbows appeared as never before. If they were not visible in the sky, we could see them reflected in the pond.

Many healings took place in this Lodge. Its sweet and gentle atmosphere grew as my mother led the rounds, tentatively at first, then with more confidence once she realized, gradually, that she had earned this right through her long years of training and fasting. Although the Lodge has since been dismantled, it will remain a hallowed and powerful spot in memory and in fact.

When Storm called to explain the mission at Diablo and invite her to take part, my mother weighed the pros and cons, overcame her reticence about political involvement and said yes. A number of us went along, following in separate cars over Walker Pass and through the canyon roads that wind to the Pacific shore. My mother's recollection of the event differs from mine only slightly. Her journal entry says:

"Driving through Walker Pass was very beautiful today. We did not know what might be ahead, what sort of confrontation, but were ready for anything the Grandfathers arranged or wanted...We arrived at the place set for the meeting to find an

empty field—everyone gone—all except a wind-up
crew, among them someone called Michael who
had heard me speak in Ojai and who directed us
to where the Deer Tribe were encamped at Morro
Bay. After debating, we decided to go there and
join them and leave a trail for the others. Just as
we drove off, Marilyn and Terry arrived. They had
been over to the beach where the action tomorrow
was to be. We all went on together to find the
Deer Tribe—and did—in a good place. We camped
together on the edge of a field. Red Eagle [an
Apache Medicine Man who had recently become a
good friend] came to welcome...Woke at dawn.
Got over to the sunrise service taking our contingent in the Tioga. The little gayly covered tents
they camped in looked touching and cosy as we
drove away. When we got there, we found a circle
forming on the beach—a very public beach and not
an attractive one. We joined the circle and everyone in it offered tobacco to the fire. Swift Turtle
made much of me as Grandmother. Red Eagle
stood beside me and I had Peter as guard of honor
with my staff.

"At the end of the sunrise service, Swift Turtle
asked me to close it. I said let us dance. And I
warmed my drum, which had gone flat, over the
fire and led a simple round, back to places. The
man from PG&E stood with me to be photo-
graphed. Then back to camp. I rested, the others
went to workshops.

"Back in the evening to beach to shoot arrows.
A lovely dance. Heymeyohsts and his drummers
and singers. Then the beautiful Pipe ceremony.
And then the four arrows were shot. I came third,

97

to the east, with Red Eagle assisting. All the arrows flew well, including mine. It was an ancient, massive bow. I hadn't shot an arrow for seventy years! But I managed, left-handed. It went straight but not far. The arrows had to be retrieved to be fired again, bearing their poems of peace, composed by the arrow maker who also shot one of the arrows with his wife as assistant. Steven and Meredith Foster.

"Then I was asked to close the gathering—and did so with a prayer—and a short song. I chose one we all, or nearly all knew, and that was that. It closed on high plane of outpouring love. Many people showered me with presents and came to the Tioga to say goodbye. I have many memories— vignettes. Terry dancing in the circle, arms outstretched—radiant. Many faces and happenings. Much joy."

My own entry reads: "For a second time I have come to see the power of nonviolent protests. This one, particularly, seems the better approach. To bless rather than curse. To love rather than mourn. Here we are, a very assorted lot—elders, children, power-people, young hippie types—and among these, the unexpected appearance of the establishment, a representative of PG&E who astonishingly took part in the sunrise circle and listened attentively to the prayers, songs and blessings. He later stood with my mother and a young man named Swift Turtle to have his picture taken. Interesting publicity, novel PR, setting a precedent perhaps for future gatherings if indeed there should be a need.

"I have such a colorful picture of us all at the ocean's edge, in the shadow of the plant and what it represents, and the earnestness with which we all took part.

"But especially, I see Eve, Grandmother to the event, being honored and revered at every turn, and the amazing strength with which she shot her arrow tonight. There were four arrows in all, one for each direction, crafted by Steven Foster, with obsidian arrowheads that I understand came from the east, south, west and northern regions of America. If that is so, what a powerful, protective shield for this spot.

"I see her stand in the center, facing east, with Red Eagle (how I've come to love and respect this man) behind her as her protector, the ocean behind him, rolling gently over the shore as a perpetual reminder of our origins, of how far we've come and how far we have yet to go, and that the tides will long caress the shores after we have all disappeared.

"The arrow shot out, straight and clear, just as the sun plunged below the horizon. It fell behind the extraordinary totem pole that had been placed in the sand for this occasion, a tall gnarled trunk of what seemed to be an exotic tree from a far away jungle, around which we danced, prayed and sang.

"A great shout went up as each arrow was unleashed, but particularly so for Eve's. It was the sight of this 79 year old, in her white buckskin tunic over her multicolored skirt, proudly standing, all 5 foot of her, a true warrior, taking her turn and giving it all that she had, sending the message that whatever comes her way she will meet it with valor and humor, that touched everyone there."

Eve and Red Eagle, Medicine Man

Steven later presented my mother with a similar arrow, and she kept it with her drum and the healing objects in her writing room. It is now on loan to Rick, my youngest son, as a steady reminder of his grandmother's spunk and straight shooting—a symbol of the paths ahead, and the one he may choose to explore.

Chapter Eleven

It was a gift from the Grandfathers that all of my children were able to see their grandmother before she left, within the period of her outward mobility and inner strength.

David and Rick had been making their appearances all along—coming up from San Diego and Ridgecrest whenever they could, together and separately—each with his own particular talent for lifting my mother's spirits. David has a natural ability to make fun of himself. He would recount in comic detail struggles with irate landlords, unrequited loves, unreasonable bosses and missed opportunities, embellishing these tales in a style calculated to make my mother laugh and to conceal his deep concern for her condition. They had always had a camaraderie with one another and shared a jocular view of life's priorities, as David well knew when he later wrote:

"There is hardly an aspect of my life that hasn't been influenced by Gran. This ranges all the way from showing me the spiritual path, total reverence for God and respect for Mother Earth, to teaching me about betting on horses. Perhaps one of her most important lessons was her sense of humor. I can hear her say over and over again how important it is to make people laugh because it brings up our human spirit....Anyone who thinks of a medicine person as being stern, unbending or humorless unfortunately never met my grandmother.

"When I think back there are so many memories that come to mind. I remember riding in the back of her Scout jeep with my younger brother Ricky and she always made sure that we each got a special treat....When I was growing up the whole family was always glad when she would come to visit and very sad to see her go. And that is where I am today, very, very sad to see her go. If I grieve, however, I grieve for myself, the rest of the family and friends, but not for her because in my heart I know she is with the Grandfathers and her spirit always will be with us. I write this now by the stream where she first shared her Pipe with me. Whenever I see a red-tailed hawk circling above, I know that she is alive in my heart as she always will be, still giving me that special wink which was just for me....."

My mother relished his visits, and when he left she would miss him "somethin' fierce," as she would say.

Rick brought music and a nonconformist outlook that my mother often empathized with and understood. Whenever he showed up she would command him to sit at the foot of her bed and sing her any or all of the songs he had composed, until his voice gave out or she fell asleep, whichever came first. They are memorable songs, melodic tunes

103

about "good medicine" and mountaintop talks with Grandfather Eagle, Wolf, Bear, Coyote and Hawk that are still sung in Sweat on occasion.

When he wasn't singing or playing his harmonica, she would sometimes ask him to retell her favorite runaway story—his experience when at age fifteen he had smuggled his best friend, a girl his age, and a large black cat aboard a Greyhound bus in Indiana, and headed for the hills of Virginia. They had set up house in an abandoned cabin near an old reservoir, and had lived there undetected for almost a week before we "rescued" them just minutes ahead of the sheriff and the girl's apoplectic parents. There was in this misadventure a certain innocence that appealed to my mother—a recognition of her childhood fantasies and flights from the grown-up world to secret places where she also had hoped she might never be found.

There was another connecting thread to these two grandsons and to a flight from reality. When they were tots of five and two, I brought them with me to California for a three-week stay with my mother who had sprung to the rescue at a time when my mind had taken a short leave of absence. ("The broken rhythm," White Eagle says. "A mini-breakdown," my friends politely called it.)

She met us in San Francisco and, concealing her anxiety about my wobbly state, she drove us down the coastline to Santa Monica in her Scout. On a whim, or so she thought at the time, she brought us to Independence a few days later. Friends of hers had recently moved there and had extended an open invitation to visit. Neither she nor they had any notion then that she would one day make Independence her home.

Her concern and support, the healing strength of the mountains, the vast open space of the high desert where accumulated stress and problems fade into insignificance—all worked together to restore my equilibrium, my sense of purpose, and I could return with the boys feeling reconnected to the world around me and in much better spirits. It was early and conclusive proof of the healing help that can come from sending a voice. My mother, having heard my cry, responded instantly. Without realizing it at the time (this happened before she became deeply involved in medicine ways) she had brought me to a place that some consider to be one of the seven power spots on our planet.

The boys came home with a lasting impression of their grandmother tooling them around in the Scout, helping them clamber over a steam engine in a small park in the town, introducing them to pinball machines, to hot dogs, to sing-alongs and unusual fairy tales from past civilizations. And now they came to give back, in their own ways, the very large helpings of love, approval and appreciation she had served up all their lives.

Soon it was John and Nancy's turn. One year into their marriage, they arrived from Indiana, just in time for the Fourth of July festivities. John, busy in his work as a Legal Services attorney (for which he had already gained some national press) had not seen his grandmother in some time, a fact they both regretted. My mother made a concerted effort to give them quality time and to enjoy their company. She was particularly proud of John's work, seeing it as an extension of her own as a healer of small and large miseries. "My grandson the lawyer and one day a Supreme Court Judge," she frequently said, with a nod of her head in his direction that scarcely concealed her respect and admiration.

She saw this visit as her golden opportunity to nudge this grandson—who strongly resembles his Canadian forebear, her father—towards something she badly wanted and thought slightly overdue. "Think baby!" she instructed them almost the moment they arrived, and many more times during their stay. "You know there are hundreds of little souls who want to come here, who want a chance to evolve and help our planet evolve. So you must begin to think about the one who will choose you above all others, [who will] come to you as a welcome guest so that you can graduate too. Mark my words!" she said, tweaking Nancy's hair.

They evidently did. Nine months later a tiny girl made her shaky debut in Indiana, and her parents named her Whitney. They insist the name is unrelated to the long day they spent alone at the Mt. Whitney portals a day or two after their arrival, but I like to think it is. Certainly, the child who had such a bumpy, tenuous beginning now gives every appearance of having absorbed many of the granitic properties and enduring qualities of the snow-capped, blue-colored peak that towers above all others on this continent.

And, in my all-too-infrequent glimpses of this child, and now her new little sister Morgan, I am struck by something else. There is a certain some-

106

thing in her bright eyes, in her impish expression, in the set of her small shoulders and sturdy little back that has the unmistakable stamp of her great-grandmother. I know this must amuse my mother, who, I feel sure, watches the development of this descendant and the growth of all her great-grand-children with affectionate curiosity and interest.

Chapter Twelve

The tiny town of Independence goes all out for its namesake celebration. There is, of course, the parade which annually consists of a rather dilapidated Mair's Market float, a couple of bright yellow firetrucks, four or five ancient relics from the American Legion marching proudly if a bit unsteadily, some ranchers on horseback, a handful of American Indians from the Fort Independence reservation, one or two mules, an ambulance and an assortment of children in costume, waving miniature flags. The procession moves solemnly up the main thoroughfare, then past the County Courthouse to the nothern edge of town, turns around and retraces its route in case someone happened to miss the first sweep of the cavalcade. It is a day in which the entire citizenry spills out, and those not in the parade make up the bulk of the small high-spirited crowd along the route.

My mother had every intention of taking her place among the spectators, and she commissioned John and Nancy to push her in a borrowed wheelchair to a vantage point in front of Pine's Cafe.

She wore a perky sun hat with red, white and blue ribbons attached, and she laughed and clapped as happily as anyone else when the parade passed by. No one watching her then could possibly have foreseen that in two weeks' time she would sail off in her own Swan Boat to join in another, more glorious parade. We might have had our suspicions a week later, but on this Fourth of July, it was the farthest thing from our minds.

There is a small airport in Independence—nothing more than a field, really, and rarely used except for the occasional private one-engine plane or as a landing spot for firefighters during seasonal brush fires—but just after twilight on the Fourth it becomes the setting for a spectacular display of fireworks.

Cars arrive from all over to line up on either side of the road so that the occupants can "oooh and aaah" at a safe distance, yet not miss the bursts of rockets as they pivot toward the sky, shatter and return to earth, much like a shower of falling stars.

My mother adored these displays and what they symbolized; she had celebrated her first Fourth of July as a proud, brand-new American citizen in Chungking, China—the land where fireworks originated. She desperately wanted to be taken that night to watch. She proposed a long rest, sleep if necessary, have someone awaken her in time to take her in the Tioga to a spot along the road, or up by my trailer where she would then perhaps camp overnight near the singing stream.

So it was approved by the committee and settled. John, Nancy and I went our ways—first to the trailer, and then as the sun dipped behind the

109

mountains, down to the road to squeeze in among
the cars, trailers and campers already in place. Certain that my mother was also among these and
was delighting in this celebration, our own enjoy-
ment was measurably heightened.

When it was over, in a final blaze of stars and
stripes, we drove back to the trailer. John and
Nancy went slightly further to where they were
staying at Marilyn Mountain's place. We said our
goodnights, and I waited for the Tioga to appear.
When, after an hour or so, it hadn't, I went to bed
assuming my mother had changed her mind and
had decided to return to the house instead.

In the morning, to my dismay, I learned that
someone had chosen to let my mother sleep
through the festivities, believing that this was in
her best interest and more important in the scheme
of things than to honor her request to attend
"America's party."

I was in a far less forgiving mood than was my
mother. After her initial disappointment on waking
to find that she had missed it all, she simply said,
"They don't understand, Terry. Let it go. Let it
be." And then she smiled a greeting to John and
Nancy, who had come with me to check on her
and let her know of their plan to go to Whitney
Portals.

This minor clash of wills and the others which
followed may have been the catalyst for what we
later called her "trial run." A week after John and
Nancy left, my mother woke from a nap to find
herself temporarily unattended, something which
had rarely, if ever, occurred. The "Palace Guard,"
as she had begun to call us, were off on various

errands or in the garden—just enough out of view to allow her to slip out of the house unnoticed, and disappear. Simply vanish. Much to her glee and to everyone else's consternation.

I hadn't been there when this happened, but I got a full report as soon as I arrived. The moment her absence was discovered a search of her most likely hiding places was conducted—the house first, and then her writing room; the little grove in the garden where, hidden from view by lilac trees and bushes, she frequently smoked her Pipe; her bedroom in her own house; and finally, almost as an afterthought, her camper, which was parked in the carport between her house and her studio.

And there she was, lying serenely in the back, blissfully lost in a Jane Austen novel, as far removed as possible from what she had begun to feel was our stifling overattentiveness and concern. It was, I think, the turning point. She may have seen, down one long road, a future of conflict between herself and others, between the outer layers and the inner resolve, between her ego and her Self. And down the other, the still waters and the waiting boat.

It was Marilyn who discovered her hiding place and had the sensitivity to keep it secret for a while before she told Iren. Iren, in turn waited ten or fifteen minutes more before going out to the camper to poke her head through the door and say, casually, in her thick Hungarian accent, "Oh there you are, darling. We were getting a little worried."

The fiercely independent Iren was one of the few who understood this small defiant act, and loved my mother for it. I did too, though I shook my head in disbelief when I realized what it had taken for my mother to get from the house, through one garden, a gate, another garden, past the Guru bath, through another gate to the camper, open the narrow door, crawl in and settle down with her beloved book. I have a feeling Jane Austen applauded.

Chapter Thirteen

There was, as it turned out, one other surreptitious get-away—just prior to the fourth and final healing Sweat—an escapade in which I played an active role.

For several days, my mother had spoken to me about the Spirit Canoe—a subject she had referred to in *The Shaman and the Medicine Wheel* as a symbol for leaving the "storms and temptations" behind to navigate fearlessly toward the promised shore. On an afternoon when I seemed to be the only one "on duty" she told me she had something to show me, and asked me to help her to her studio. "No one needs to know about this," she said, giving my arm a conspiratorial squeeze. "It will be just 'us girls.' "

I hung a Do Not Disturb sign on the door and we stepped out together, taking time, first, to watch a hummingbird flit purposefully among the hollyhocks, to stare at distant cloud formations above the valley and to pause for a moment at her small sacred grove with its circle of rocks and a large crystal geode in the center. We covered the distance between the house and the studio at a slow, even pace. At length we were in the familiar room with its rows of books, shelves of musical tapes and accumulated papers.

She had brought a Pipe bag along and a small box, and she asked me to put these on the Navajo rug on the floor and then to help her sit. I took my place beside her, to her left, where she indicated she wanted me to be. She opened the box with great care and took out three smooth white stones—one small, grey, slightly humpbacked rock with the face of a dolphin; a luminous shell; and a tiny carved swan. She had me position these along the rug, and then asked me to reach for the figure of a Medicine Man that Raymond had carved for her, which she kept on her desk.

This was one of his earliest "whittlings," as he calls his ingenuous carved figures. It stands about four inches high, with its arms raised in benediction and an expression on its face that alternates between being slightly stern to kind and approving, depending on one's point of view or the reflection of light. She had me place it at the front end of the rug, facing out, with its strong straight back toward us.

"Now we're all set," she said when everything had been put just so. "You see the pattern on this rug? How it comes to a point in the front and back? And how the sides go out like a canoe? This is my Spirit Canoe. I sit like this, close my eyes and imagine I'm taking off on a still, quiet lake, or sometimes, when I'm really adventurous, the sea. I use this before I start my work, especially my

114

writing, and I want you to know more about it now so that when it comes time to do your own book you'll have this as an additional and powerful tool.''

She told me to close my eyes and see what came to mind. ''Ladies in the stern,'' I said, and we laughed, remembering a time in Nova Scotia when our good friend Captain John Casey, an old salt and my surrogate grandfather, had barked this order after helping us aboard his new, modernly equipped fishing boat. At other times, when we had shared some dangerous adventures on the Bay of Fundy in his perilously small and antiquated trawler, he had never shown any special concern over our seating arrangements, so this sudden protective attitude had come as a complete surprise.

I closed my eyes. After a moment I felt as though we were being gently launched on a slow current of water—a river (''the river she is flowing, down to the sea'') or a calm brown lake from my childhood. There was a sense of shores receding, and the sound of oars dipping in and out.

Other images floated up: a flying fish I had seen once, after a night of the ''doldrums'' on a friend's trimaran, ten miles off the California coast. (I've never understood this sailor's term. Far from being in the doldrums, I was overjoyed to spend the night adrift, on fluorescent water, and to wake to the sight of the flying fish and a school of porpoise playing around and beneath the boat. I thought it terribly romantic. My navigator, an attorney on a tight schedule, did not exactly share my enthusiasm.)

After the flying fish came whales, the blue ones

of the Bay of Fundy and the grey we watch migrating off the San Diego coast.

And then a series of water images returned. Tidal pools left behind in the crevices of dark grey rocks and coves beneath the cliffs at Victoria Beach, where I used to spend hours watching the microcosmic world of snails, darting minnows, seaweed weaving sinuously to and fro. I saw cascading waterfalls and wind-driven streams. I saw a deep clear canal banked on either side by masses of flowers and lush green trees, a buried memory of England perhaps.

Now faces began to form, recent and old friends, some of whom had already gone on but appeared again as I had first known them. One of these was the face of a young girl named Smitty, the most beautiful girl I had ever known, who had befriended me my first year in America at Walnut Hill and who came to spend part of the summer holiday with me before we went on to our separate colleges. The next year, when she was seventeen, she died of a particularly vicious and rapid form of cancer, and I was left, in our young friendship, with intense memories of summer nights spent reading poetry aloud (usually Dorothy Parker and Edna St. Vincent Millay, since we saw ourselves as being equally worldly-wise and cynical about the ways of "men"), of plotting exotic futures as we smoked forbidden cigarettes, of wallowing in shared symptoms of unrequited love—heartaches caused by two local Adonises whose indifference and nonchalance toward our hero worship only made them all the more attractive. Remembering those times, for a split second I relived that sharp

116

sensation of being so much in love one can't think beyond the next breath or even care if there will be one.

Her death was my first lesson in separation, apart from the "small deaths" I had felt during my long absences from home and at age sixteen I had found it almost impossible to accept. How could a *loving* God take such a vital, funny, bright and quixotic girl before she had even had a taste of the fruits of life?

"Tears are for the living," I remember my mother telling me then. "Smitty has completed her work this time around and she was given added insurance. She met the challenge with courage and light, and she passed all the tests. She doesn't have to go through them ever again. She is immortal as we all are, so she will always be here, but she is also *there*, in a far, far better place. She's free."

The wisdom of those words came back to me now. I had a better understanding of them, though it was many years before I could replace my opinion of an unfair deity with a picture of an all-knowing, benevolent Creator who has a master plan for all of us.

All the faces that flashed before me were of people, young and old, good and bad, who have made a difference on my voyage. Yet as suddenly as they arrived, they disappeared again, like the "whirlies" we sometimes see at a distance, the dustwinds that spontaneously churn up the earth and then die away without a trace.

Now came a flood of music—birds singing, crows calling, an eagle's shrill whistling, a boys' choir—a

117

Eve at Deep Springs College

symphony of sound over which I could also hear my mother's distinct voice in prayer. These sounds built up to a crescendo and faded away to a penetrating silence. And then we were, as at the beginning, cutting across mirrored glass, two shadowy figures in a silver bark canoe with our red catlinite guide at the prow.

I was suddenly overcome by what the French call "tristesse," that bittersweet sadness for which I haven't an equivalent English term, of being deeply touched, of unleashing a long-held sympathy for the human condition, of a heart splitting with love for the human spirit. Hot tears formed. I opened my eyes to find my mother looking at me with compassion.

"I know," she said. "It's not a journey to be taken lightly. You'll need to go very slowly on this one—as on all others. But it will bring you much peace as you practice it, and the greatest joy. Not only will it help you with your work, but when the time comes to take the boat and keep on going, you'll have the courage and strength to face whatever and whoever is waiting out there. The Great Committee."

She patted my hand and added, "You know I'll be there too, to welcome you. You needn't worry about that."

I nodded, blinking back my tears, and tried to smile.

"Poor lamb," said my mother. "Just when you thought you might escape? But we've been together far too many times to separate now." We laughed together, releasing our pent-up melancholy. I helped her put the stones and the small

119

swan back into their box and placed the pipestone figure on its shelf. I watched as she carefully wrapped the Pipe she had used, in its rabbit skin bag. When she had secured it tightly, she sat for a long moment, rubbing her hand along the grey and brown fur. She turned to face me.

"Here," she said, suddenly handing me the bag. "I want you to have this. It's to be used with the canoe. I have been keeping this Pipe to use only for my work, my writing. I have been thinking about another book and I want you to write it with me. If I'm not able to finish it, then you'll have the Pipe and the canoe to carry it on. I know you can do it, don't look so dismayed! Keep and guard the Pipe, and then when we get started, we'll smoke it together, here, in this room, and who knows where it will take us."

We walked back in silence, the soft fur of the Pipe bag brushing against my arm as we moved. No one had seen us go. Our journey had lasted only a few minutes, but as I helped my mother into her bed and we waited for the others to appear, I knew when we winked at each other we had been gone for an eternity.

Chapter Fourteen

Another matter my mother wanted settled was my fast. She had accepted my initial postponement, but now she urged me to set up another date and not to let anything interfere. I promised I would.

A day or two later I drove to Big Pine to see Raymond. He was waiting for me in the yard, not far from his small frame home where, amid the delectable wafts of food coming from the kitchen, we often found Evalina and him surrounded by grandchildren.

We sat on a couple of worn chairs beneath a tall cottonwood that cast its shade around us and over a vegetable garden a few feet beyond. Two or three chickens scratched in the nearby dirt, and several kittens crept out of hiding places in the woodpile to watch us in curiosity, then scamper away. There was no one else in sight. A horse whinnied in the distance, and a large grey hawk circled overhead.

"Well," Raymond said in his familiar drawl, after looking me over for a long time. "What you got to say for yourself?"

In the presence of this old friend and teacher I grew suddenly shy. I looked down at my feet and stared at some ants crawling slowly over my sandals. Then I looked up. "It's about my fast," I said. "With everything that's been going on, I wonder if we could set up another time."

"What do you want to fast for?" Raymond asked, not unkindly. It was part of the ritual to ask me again and have me answer, so that he could "check it out" to see if I still had a good reason.

"I want to find my direction," I said in a loud voice. Raymond's hearing has deteriorated over the years, and my voice is not in the range he hears best on a human level. He has no trouble hearing the other voices that direct his work. "I want to fast for my purpose," I continued. "To know what my work will be, and how I can best help others."

"Ah ha," he said. "Your purpose." And he reached into his plaid shirt pocket for a cigarette, which I knew he would smoke as another part of the ritual.

"Yes, that's it," I answered, and laughed at the absurdity of a woman my age (the age of vintage wine, as someone once tactfully put it) not knowing her purpose. Raymond laughed too, a loud "ha!" that set the chickens to clucking and flapping their stunted wings. And then he lit the cigarette and offered the smoke to the four directions. After a thoughtful pause he said, "Well. That's good. You come in September. We'll put you in then. We'll do our talking first of the month, and then we'll see."

I knew "our talking" meant telling him again why I wanted to fast and what I should do and

122

bring with me at that time. I thanked him for this and for the help his Sweats had brought my mother.

"See you on Saturday," I told him. "That's the final one."

"Yes. And you tell my old friend that I'll have something to say to her when she comes."

I drove back to Independence and told my mother how it had gone, and gave her Raymond's message. I said that I liked the idea of a September fast, since it was my favorite time of the year and my birthday month. She was reassured by the news, and told me she had only worried that Raymond's heavy schedule and the amount of travelling he was doing might have prevented me from taking part.

"Not to worry," I said. "It's all settled. And you'll be my 'family.' I only hope I can go through it half as well as you did."

"You'll sail through, I know you will," she answered, smiling happily. "And I'll be right there with you. One way or another."

Later that night I dug through a box of letters from my mother that I kept in my trailer and found the one I wanted to look at again. I sat at my kitchen table next to the wide window that overlooked the stream, and as it rushed by in the dark, I read:

"Darling. I am not sure where to begin this account of the first two nights of the Fast. I went up early on Friday afternoon and Raymond was making the fire for the Sweat before 'putting me in.'

"I watched a small eagle come from the south and fly over his head. A moment later he pointed up to it and said, 'It will come back. A small eagle.'

"The Sweat was wonderful and well attended. The young things from Mammoth had come down, four of them, in a little VW, with a foot or more of snow on its roof. They took over and did all the sweeping and getting ready of the community hall, and the food, etc. And helped with the fire.

"Then it became time to put me in, and Raymond did so around 9:30. He smudged me with sweet grass, punkum, and filled my Pipe and stuffed it with sage so that I should not smoke it until early Sunday morning, though I might hold it if I needed to.

"It was on a bed of sage beside my head when I lay down, but first, of course, I sat up as long as I could, praying and chanting, and thinking.

"It was not a total blackness inside, the Grandfathers were kind to my claustrophobia and left a dim sort of lavender glow, not bright enough to see anything, but comforting.

"I prayed for everything in my Pipe and lots of other things and people. In the Sweat, I had been asked to state what I was fasting for and I told them 'for more power in this Sweat Lodge and a blessing for Raymond and his family, and for more power to help the people'... by that I meant more power in my own Pipe.

"After a long while, the lavender light faded, and two wheels of bright golden light appeared, one where Raymond sits and one where Paul sits, on either side of the door. They were brilliant, and flashing, and had sparklers round the rims. They stayed there for awhile, then one of them went out, and the other circled the lodge, then it too went out, and the dark cold night began.

"After another long time I lay down, still keeping awake, and praying aloud, etc....and so the night passed.

"In the morning Raymond came to let me out, to say my first prayer to the Grandfather, hands upward to the east (and then a visit to the outhouse!) and then I returned to my fast lodge for the long, long day. In the afternoon, as I told you on the telephone, a flock of small blackbirds with white eyes came round the altar outside the Sweat lodge where Raymond puts his Pipe, and where we pick up the sage before we go in, and they went over the top of it, and round about, and peeked in as they passed the opening, which was very small, of the lodge. Then they stopped chattering and disappeared, and after a pause an enormous magpie went by, fat and lustrous, and with something that looked like a crown on his head. I never saw one quite like that. Part of him reminded me of the pictures I have seen of hoopoes.

"That was all that day, except for my thoughts and rememberings, and deciding what to pray for when night came.

"Raymond put me in again around seven this time with a more elaborate ceremonial for the second night, and Paul came in to assist. Raymond was working with flaming sweet grass and he did a sort of ritual dance with it and smudged everything many times, flashing it across my eyes, and my ears, and my head, and my Pipe, over and

over. Then he and Paul sat silent for a long time
and I too, and then they went and I was fastened
in for the long black night.

"It grew bitterly cold. It was the coldest night
we have had so far and my sleeping bag was thin.
Even with Edie's magnificent red blanket I was
very cold. But this kept me awake and I sat up
and prayed and chanted. . . . Then after what must
have been some hours, the visions began.

"This time there were small, fiery clouds, not
like the little lights we often see in the Sweat
lodge, but big as a hand, and floating about the
place, in a sort of dance, rather like Raymond's.
That lasted for a time, and then faces began, many
many faces, finally settling in a row opposite me,
and stretching out indefinitely through the wall
and into space.

"Most were Indian, but there were some white.
They looked very serious at first, especially the
front row, which all looked like your description of
the man on television [Mad Bear—a chief who had
come to Kentucky to protect burial grounds that
were being excavated—whom I had written about
to my mother] except that they wore blankets over
their heads instead of his regalia, and no one
seemed more eminent than anyone else. Presently
some of them smiled, and then they began to
disappear.

"I thanked them for coming, and prayed some
more, until I lost my voice and could only whis-
per. I lay down, and then a lot of pain came to
me, my back (I think perhaps the kundalini was
being treated, the chakras opened a little more)
and this, added to the cold and the impossibility of
getting comfortable, kept me awake, except that

now and then I blacked out, and I think went travelling, to you. And to others.

"The young people in Mammoth were holding a Pipe meeting for me and one of them who is really clairvoyant said that I was suddenly with them, near enough to be touched. He told me this on Sunday morning, after I came out. I knew I wasn't asleep because I had no sense of having failed, which you do have, if you sleep, so I conclude I blacked out and went out of body to do certain things, and visit people.

"Several have called to say they were very conscious of me over the weekend. Margaret Baker, who didn't know I was fasting, said she suddenly felt sure I must be, though it was the 'wrong time of year' in her mind. And Margaret Phillips—you remember her, the bright light in Bishop whom I admire so much and who sent me that touching note."

[My mother is referring here to a note Margaret sent her after she had read Mary Austin's *The Children Sing in the Far West* aloud to her children. Margaret quoted her son as saying: "It sounds as if it was written by a pretty lady. Was she pretty? What did she look like?" And Margaret had replied that Mary Austin was not pretty in the everyday use of that word, but that she looked like a fine person with a beautiful soul. Her son then said he meant pretty "like a lady who would be outdoors and wear pants and ride a horse like that lady who used to live in the house on the creek in Lone Pine."

"Do you mean Evelyn Eaton?"

"Yes." That's who he had meant. That was the kind of pretty he had in mind. Like Evelyn Eaton.]

127

"[Margaret] wrote that she was very conscious of me arriving, and told me to read Isaiah 40, verse 31 which she said was written especially for me. So you might want to borrow one of the many Bibles at Wavertree [The Virginia Center for Creative Arts, where I had been accepted as a writer for a three-week stay] and read it to the group.

"All the time as I lay in blackness and the pain, which was intense, a small eagle—I am almost sure it was the same one we saw—sat beside my head and comforted me. So I knew everything was alright.

"And indeed when I came out at dawn and saw the dear men making the fire, and shivering... having to get up at four to come from Mammoth and Deep Springs, I felt very cherished. Raymond had put some hot stones in my camper for me to change, sweet man, and that did help. I could only crawl out on my hands and knees but presently I was able to stand and go back and smoke my Pipe while I watched them through the open doorway, tending to the fire.

"Then the Sweat and my report, after Paul who ran it had given his, and Raymond his, on how he found all well when he took me out and that the Spirits had been to his house and woken him by calling his name, and he had thought it was his wife but she said she hadn't called. So we went through Sweat, and then the eating and lots of talk with everyone so very sweet to me.

"I was very intrigued in the Sweat when Helen [Helen Maghee, a Paiute elder and longtime friend who originally gave my mother the name 'Mahad'yuni'] went into a long and magic Paiute

Helen Maghee, Pauite elder, Eve, Lillian Baker, Pauite basket weaver and beadworker (Photo by Louise Kelsey)

prayer spattered with 'Evieleenies' as she calls me in Paiute and then said in English that the 'whirlies are not from our Mother, whirlies come for Evieleenie, something special from her Grandfathers and her Mother....' Helen sat next to me at the opening Sweat and when I reported on the pain said, 'She is trying to tell us, she is crying,' which I nearly was, and then she added, 'You will be brave, go through well, all four nights.' Which I hope to do.

"And that's about it darling. You can relay what you like of this. Thank everyone for me and say that I did indeed feel all their thoughts and help and that they were well remembered and prayed for so that each should receive a special blessing.

"Tell them if there is anything they especially want me to tell the 'whirlies' to let me know before Friday.

"Best love to you and I hope the writing goes well as it seems to have started."

I had, of course, read the accounts of her fasts in *I Send a Voice* and had gained much helpful insight from these. But this letter spoke to me on a more personal level, and I referred to it several times before I was "put in" for my own fast in September, as planned, just slightly less than two months after my mother had gone on. I did sail through it, and true to her word, she sent me many signs that she was with me throughout those long and extraordinary days and nights.

A fast is a very private experience, a communion between one's self, the Grandfathers and God. A suspended period of time in which everything is stripped away, all pretense, all self-deception. One

130

is in the presence of the Spirits as on no other occasion, with the exception of a Vision Quest or possibly at the moment of birth, when the naked, vulnerable, innocent human being is about to take her first breath on the voyage.

All that I am permitted to say about my fast now, or perhaps ever, is that I was told many things, I had visions, and I was accompanied throughout by loving, caring and supportive beings. I hope never to forget those long dark nights and hot days, and that I will hold on to the answers I received. I *can* say that I emerged with a new sense of purpose, with a renewed commitment to my work in the theatre as an instrument for light and healing, a concept I had thought about and now understand more completely.

I know my mother was there, urging me on all the way. I know she was proud. For one exalted moment in an experience very similar to hers, I felt at one with the stars.

Chapter Fifteen

To complete the cycle begun with the first of my mother's healing Sweats, it was now time for the fourth and final one. Everything in fours, always, to honor the four directions and all that they represent.

My mother had come to the first, weak and debilitated, unable to breathe without the oxygen tank and unable to walk. Now, as we readied ourselves for this sweat, she stood unaided and unafraid at the entrance, then stoically took her place inside next to Raymond, who had her stretch out along the northeast wall.

"Everybody ready?" Everybody was. Or thought they were. We had seen such steady, miraculous progress that we could only look forward to more as we began our prayers and chants with renewed energy and hopes.

White Eagle says: "God did more than give man this beautiful Earth to live on, this beautiful body for the spirit to inhabit. Throughout the ages He has sent messengers to help him. In the beginning messengers came to this planet not only from the spirit world but from other planets and from outer space....They came to bring man the vision glorious; to give him knowledge of the universal and celestial life....One day man will realize that he is surrounded, not only by the spirit worlds and beings, but by the finer physical or semi-physical worlds inhabited by people similar to himself. Mingling with you sometimes are spirits not of this world but from other planets to speak through a sensitive human instrument. Man is set in his ideas, and cannot get away from his one-track mind. But beyond that one-track mind are so many wonderful things, a glorious life of which you know nothing. You find life difficult and lonely, and you feel as though you are always toiling; your feet are heavy and the road along which you drive yourself grows very hard. But learn to open your vision and have courage to *believe what you want to believe.*"

Closed in the comfort of that dark, warm and moist womb, in harmony with our Sweat sisters and brothers (we are asked to leave all negativities outside the Lodge, not to bring in discord or envy or mistrust or any of our darker and lower plane habits) it is easier to accept and understand, sometimes even to see, the rainbow bridge between the spirit world and our human experience.

What I wanted to believe, and did believe, was that the best and right answers would come for my mother, and that she would be given the strength to meet them fearlessly and with the same integrity with which she had met all her other challenges. That meant, I hoped, that she would stay with us for a long time, and would continue to

133

teach, to lead, to learn and to help, as she had always helped, with humor and compassion.

We had a book to do, we would work together, we would smoke the Pipe in the Spirit Canoe. We would—as a talented young composer named Fox had once suggested after seeing the close bond between us—begin a workshop for families and set an example of how each generation could take part, from the great-grandmother down to the smallest member. There was so much to look ahead to, so much to be done.

Midway through the Sweat which was hotter and more strenuous than the others, Raymond spoke up after a very long prayer. "You have a choice," he said very loudly. "You can stay or you can go. It's up to you. But you have to tell Those Above what you want. *You* have to tell *them*. You understand?"

After a long pause, my mother answered. "Yes, I understand. It's not easy for me to tell the Grandfathers what I want. I still have that old notion that it's presumptuous, but I know I must. I've been confused. Sometimes I have felt I want it to go one way, sometimes another. But what I do want, most of all, is to be able to say 'it is finished in beauty,' and to move forward, bravely, toward the light."

There was another long pause. Then, in the courteous manner and traditional way we have been taught to always ask permission before we talk, my mother said, "Raymond, may I speak?"

"Ho! Speak away."

She began a long and moving prayer of thanks for all the help she had received, and for her long years of friendship with Raymond, bumpy as they had sometimes been, and for his family. She asked blessings on "each and every one of us," and told us to continue our work of being bridges. To say yes to every mission that came our way. To remember our spirit guides and our power animals, and to give offerings to these as she had been taught to do, and not to forget that they are always with us, through the good and through the bad.

She reminded us to "take the elevator," and lift ourselves above the petty squabbles and draining difficulties of our everyday lives. She asked for a clear mind, for "strength, wisdom and understanding" of Raymond's words, and she asked forgiveness for any real or imagined offenses she might have caused along the way. She said she thought the time had come for her to step down, to retire, so that others could step forward to carry on the work.

She closed the prayer with an outpouring of love for Mother Earth and all her inhabitants. She asked again for a blessing on all her relatives, past and present. She concluded with a resounding "ho!" and a request for the river song.

In thin and wavering voices we offered up, "The river she is flowing, flowing and growing/The river she is flowing, down to the sea./Mother carry me, child I will always be/Mother carry me down to the sea." And then Raymond asked for individual songs. Some were very beautiful and sung especially for my mother. When it was my turn I sang "Amazing Grace," never imagining that four years later I would sing all the verses in a Broadway show, and that each night of the run, as I sang it, I would remember the Lodge and my mother's last Sweat.

There were more chants and prayers and then it was over. My mother went straight to the Tioga and did not stay for the community supper. We drove her home and tucked her into bed, where she lay, tired to the marrow but utterly serene.

She had made her decision and only the Grandfathers knew what it was.

Chapter Sixteen

In a few days' time, I had a far less sweeping decision to make, but nevertheless an important one. We had been handed a rare and exceptional opportunity to develop and hone our skills as caretakers, to be teachers even as we were perennial students and to reach for the highest level of good. With my mother's cooperation, endorsement and encouragement we had managed, for the most part, to overcome what at the start might have seemed insurmountable obstacles. Our mission had been to fully support my mother, to assuage her pain, to strengthen her faith as well as our own, and to bring her as much cheer, dignity and hope as we humanly could. That was our purpose, to love and care for someone whose life and example had changed, lifted and affected so many.

We used every tool at our command. Music, literature, prayers, chants, massage, crystals, western medicine, herbs, sacred healing feathers and the ever-widening circle of loyal friends, students and healers in faraway places who joined their petitions to our own.

We found we could soar to unimaginable heights and occasionally to some unfortunate depths. In a compressed amount of time we had tapped the range of every known human emotion, and there was great joy in this and proportionate sadness. Above all, in this gift from the Grandfathers of our time together, there was the golden opportunity to give back in kind. We put into practice all that we knew, all that my mother had taught us, drawing from her own accumulated knowledge, not only from Native American traditions but from many other sources—Buddhist, Christian, Celtic, Comasonic—around the Wheel. Collectively, we strove to serve as instruments of the Light.

It wasn't always easy. We slipped and flubbed more than once. As my mother's purpose became more clearly defined, a certain amount of friction developed which my mother felt was directed at her by one of the caretakers. While this may have been true, it was probably due more to that particular stage of denial which often precedes acceptance of death (as has been described by Dr. Elisabeth Kübler-Ross—a long time admirer of my mother's work and an occasional vistor—in her masterful book *On Death and Dying*) than to a willful desire to upset my mother. I was often caught in the middle and, as can happen to "bridges," there was an accompanying sense of pain and confusion, a fact my mother understood and knew very well. So, I decided to absent myself in the hope that this might provide the caretaker and my mother a freer atmosphere for more direct communication and reconciliation.

I went to San Diego to see one of my closest

friends, Lani, who had stayed with me on occasion and who had taken part in a gay and spontaneous birthday party for Iren in June which my mother had asked us to arrange as a pay-back for all her loyal, selfless contributions.

It had given Lani a chance to see for herself the holistic setup and the results which I had been reporting every so often. My mother counselled her privately, as she did any visitor who requested it, and reminded Lani to keep up her guard, to wear her shield and to "go shining" on her way. I knew that if I turned to Lani now she would offer me her support and understanding, and she did.

I called Independence from Lani's house as soon as I arrived, and was told that my mother was sitting on the porch of her own home, playing cards (a form of Russian solitaire she had learned from her father and had taught us all to play). I was overjoyed to hear this. It all sounded so normal, so plausible, so like the old days when, as a daily ritual, my mother and Iren (and anyone else who happened by) would take an afternoon break to play "the game," swap stories, have tea and relax before returning to studios and homes. Most people learned to arrive at this time, since it was a rare opportunity to find both Iren and Eve together and free to talk.

Indeed, never one to miss an opportunity to bring the Grandfathers in, my mother frequently used these breaks to encourage visitors to open up about their difficulties or problems, so she could spring into action on their behalf.

"The game" was often used as a subterfuge if a guest wasn't familiar with my mother's teachings.

It provided a safe environment for subjects which might not otherwise have been brought to light.

My mother could also read the cards, a gift she inherited from her own mother, who had been taught by gypsies. Although she sometimes hesitated, knowing what the cards could reveal, she seldom refused requests, particularly when pestered by visiting grandchildren. Her predictions were uncannily accurate. She never misused the gift. She always asked for both permission and protection, and if she saw something that might be upsetting, she tried as prudently as possible to advise the person that the difficulty ahead was really just another opportunity for growth.

Filled with warm memories of these companionable afternoons, I went straight to the beach and plunged into the ocean. After a time, feeling thoroughly at peace, I strolled along the water's edge, disturbing sandpipers in the process, and picked up small shells to examine and put back. Scooping handfulls of wet sand, I suddenly saw a large mottled shell at my feet, similar to a conch, which echoes the sound of the sea when held close to the ear. It is very rare to come across such a shell on San Diego beaches; I took it as a sign from the sea, a gift for my mother. I thanked the Grandfathers, and having nothing else to give at the time I made an offering of a penny I found in my swimsuit pocket.

This was another of my mother's teachings, and an ingrained Native American custom. One should never remove an object from its location without first asking permission and then giving something in return, usually tobacco or corn. It's such a tiny

gesture of appreciation and, when faithfully practiced, a very humbling reminder of our place in the
order of things in which, in Native American tradition, we are all equal.

On the following day I phoned again, and my
mother answered. She told me she was feeling
particularly well and was on good terms with
everyone. Hearing this, I knew I could come back.
I told her I would return the next day, in time, I
hoped, for the regular Sweat. We had an easy conversation and, as always, an exchange of love and
goodbyes.

I headed for home the next afternoon, later than
planned. A chance meeting with a director had detained me, but it was good news for my future
career, which I knew would cheer my mother.
She, in the meantime, had spent the day making a
number of long distance calls to close personal
friends, among them Wabun and Dr. G. She left
various instructions with caretakers for me, and
she dictated a list of items she wanted people to
have as remembrances.

Sometime during the afternoon she had removed
the White Eagle ring from her finger. It had been
sent to her years before by a channel for White
Eagle who had read *The Trees and Fields Went the
Other Way* and felt that it should go to my mother
for safekeeping. She now ceremoniously presented
it to Edie.

A stranger—a registered nurse whose life work is
with the terminally ill—arrived, for unknown
reasons, and I was later told that my mother had
greeted her as the "Daughter of Death," for whom
she had been waiting.

141

My mother spent the rest of the day in the garden, surrounded by caretakers and friends. She listened to Iren's tapes, read aloud, talked quietly and joked amiably. She was at peace with herself, with those around her and ''all her relatives'' on Mother Earth. Toward sunset she sent the caretakers off to Sweat with messages of love for Raymond and a fond farewell.

It was perhaps her most carefully planned and generous give-away that I knew nothing of this as I drove through the desert at dusk with my news and the shell. As I climbed toward the Sierra Nevadas I sang to the evening star making its first appearance above them, and knew only that I felt happy and optimistic. A lone crow called to me from its perch on a telephone pole as I drove past.

''One crow sorrow,'' I called back, ''watch it out of sight...'' and I sped on through the darkening valley.

Four days later, in a small private ceremony in the garden, we clustered about the sacred grove as Iren played my mother's favorite Brahms lullaby on her concert piano, leaving the door open so that the music flowed through us. We read from the works of Donne, Keats, Shelley and other favorite poets, passages from the Bible and from the writings of White Eagle. I scattered a portion of ashes among the roses, beneath the statue of Saint Francis, in the grove and outside the studio.

In September, soon after my fast, a greater number of people gathered at the Medicine Wheel to pay further tribute and to share personal vignettes and memories of my mother's life and influence.

Raymond arrived with two Medicine Men to lead us in strong chants and prayers. A child wandered away from the Wheel and came running back with a red-tail hawk feather that had fallen to the ground from one of the ancient oak trees.

David and Rick stood on either side of me and offered touching eulogies along with the others. As before there were all types and ages of people, each with something uniquely theirs to recall and to share. Among these were Robert and Mary Dane who, several months before, had lifted my mother's professional spirits by negotiating a contract for film rights to *Go Ask the River*. There was a double-edged poignancy as Robert, quoting Li T'ai Po, said, "Go ask the river which are longer, the eastward flowing waters or the thoughts that fill us at this parting hour."

With Raymond at my side, I walked to a place just north of the Wheel to scatter the remainder of my mother's ashes among the sagebrush and thickets of wild rose. A sudden, swift gust of wind whirled around and above us. I shook my head and smiled. "She never could stay in one place," I said to Raymond. "She's flying with the wind."

"That's right," Raymond answered. "She's doing her dance. She's happy now. She's free."

Chapter Seventeen

In my flight with crows over the landscape, the trees and fields of my mother's life and especially her last few months, I have purposefully re-created these scenes in general rather than specific terms. In keeping with Native American tradition as I've been taught it and am still learning, respectful silence is often more clearly heard than long-winded, analytical, sometimes erroneous exposés of Medicine Power approaches to spiritual healing in life and in afterlife.

If, in our circle through sorrow, mirth, weddings, birth, secrets told and untold, a picture of my mother's courage, warmth, wit, faith, imagination and, above all, commitment to the Great Spirit emerges, then my efforts will have been deeply rewarded in spite of some of the difficulties—or hazards in flight—I sometimes had to face in putting together this travelogue.

Her own books—as scores of letters on file at Boston University's Mugar Memorial Library and at my home attest—have been, and will continue to be, genuinely inspired sources of light, wonder, compassion and healing, an awesome legacy for which we will always be grateful.

My original intention had been to publish excerpts from this overwhelming collection and entitle the book *Letters to Grandmother*. But not long ago I had come to Independence to dismantle the studio, distribute some of my mother's belongings and pack the rest away. One afternoon I sat in the swivel chair at her desk and faced the west windows as she had so often done. I saw her there again, flashing her mischievous smile, waving and beckoning to me to come in, come in, as I walked toward her from the garden. I would interrupt her work for a few stolen moments of "catching up with the dear Queen," as her grandmother put it, or simply bask in one another's company.

The last of the boxes had been packed and labeled, a difficult and exhausting labor of love. For one last time, I told myself, I will "lift up mine eyes unto the hills" and ask a blessing on this empty studio, the garden, the grove and all the remaining ghosts. As I said my final amen, seven crows flew by the window. They circled from east to south, from south to west, and in a tight formation they disappeared from view on their way north. *Joy Before Night* got its start at that moment.

From sorrow to joy, from wolf to swan, from porcupines to teddy bears, the "little black eagles" have escorted me throughout the passages of this book. It has been written primarily to honor the one who walked in balance on our Mother Earth, who took her place on the Wheel and danced around its rim in harmony and in humility, with humor and with honesty. Her truth, as so many who were drawn to it found, was in the simple, tranquil, direct and reverent manner in which she heard the call of the Grandfathers. And in the generous, open-hearted way she passed on their message.

I believe the best illustration of this comes from one of my mother's talks at the close of a large gathering sponsored by the Bear Tribe in northern California in 1982. In gratitude to all who loved her, all who gave her their generous support through their prayers and friendship, and because it is only fitting, my mother now has the last word.

I exit, stage left. I leave behind a picture of Evelyn Eaton, nearly eighty, dressed in white buckskin with an intricate beaded shawl around her shoulders, made especially for her by a direct descendent of Wovoka. Blue medallions hang from her ears, and on her feet, a pair of soft leather moccasins. She stands before a microphone, alone on a wide stage at the foot of a dell, while the audience is seated on a steep slope. She is leaning on her walking stick, sometimes called her talking stick, and though she seems frail there is, in the smile she throws to the crowd, a visible, enduring strength.

She begins:

''I believe we can take away from here many new and old ideas, and reinforcements, and reassurances, and confirmations of the different ways we're going toward the Great Spirit.

''I believe that we can have a better understanding of other people's ways and much more appreciation of our own ways.

''I believe we can build on the old traditions that

have been handed down to us and so generously shared by Native American Medicine Men and Women, that have been treasured and brought through great difficulties and dangers in order to be given to us. And these they have given us at the same time that they share their most sacred traditions, as we saw at the great Pipe ceremony here, yesterday. They have also given us their trust that we will be worthy of their sharing, that we will be able to reverence and respect the traditions and be sure that we reverence our own Pipes and our own selves as being entrusted with them, and also to build on these, also to grow with these.

"Because everything is changing, everything is growing. Even the Great Spirit is not static. Wankun Tanka is growing, growing, and our own growth is part of that. We are each needed, really desperately needed, to stand firm, to live up to the very best and highest that we know in order that the Great Spirit above may grow. Our growth is needed for theirs. It's a wonderful thought. It does change our ideas about our place in the universe.

"So I think we take away from here many pictures, many memories of bridges being built, friends meeting old friends, friends making new friends, children, older people, young ones, all sorts of happenings.

"I was privileged and honored to be called grandmother by so many new grandchildren—new to me—and it is always an honor to be called grandmother, as it is to be called granddaughter or grandson. We have forgotten those ways, but they were very strong in the old days.

[sound of crow calling]

147

"Grandfather Crow is assenting to this, making me feel that I'm saying what the Grandfathers like to have said.

"Also, I was privileged, while I was here this time, to assist in a wedding. I always want to cry at weddings because I think they are terribly sad. [laughter] Terribly difficult. I think marriage is one of the most difficult tests, the most tormenting tests that the Grandfathers and the Lords of Karma have ever invented for us. [much laughter]

"It is also a very wonderful way to grow. I mean, it does make us grow if we succeed in building a marriage. That is the most beautiful and enduring thing. Very few people even try to build a marriage. They feel that the *wedding* is the marriage and that after that they can begin to quarrel right away. [laughter] [pause] Legally, or something. [laughter drowns out the next few words]

"The rainbow bridge must be made between people who get married. It must be made between parents and children, it must be made between children and grandparents. Between friends, between tribes, between nations.

"As you know, the rainbow in the sky was a promise, we are told in the Bible in the Christian way of doing things. It was God's promise to the earth, but He only gave a half of the bow. It is for us to build the circle of the bow underneath. When we get that completed by the light, by the rainbow lights in our lives, then we have the whole rainbow circle and then things will be very different.

"So, the building of bridges, the making of friendships, *dancing* together like last night, singing together many times, all this is very important.

"Wankun Tanka is the Deity of JOY. Of joy and lightness, and of song and dance. And of everything that is beautiful and is lovely and heart-lifting.

"And one of the very important disciplines we have, one of the pleasing rituals, is once a day at least, to make someone laugh in a kind way. Laughter is the great medicine but jeering laughter is the reverse. Now, if you can't find anyone on earth to make laugh, make yourself laugh.

"Laughter is a wonderful remedy. And I know that there have been occasions on these two marvelous days that we have been privileged to be here where there have been reasons for tears. Happy tears and sad tears, and these tears have been good. They have enriched our Mother Earth. They open up...you know, 'the river she is flowing,' the song says, and 'mother carry me down to the sea.'

"Tears are good, but laughter is even more important, I feel, because it's more rare. We seem to be growing through suffering, growing through sorrow. That's *our* fault. [laughter]

"If we would grow when the sun shines...well, you all know what happens when the sun shines, we lie down and get a suntan and we don't do anything that day. [laughter]

"So the Grandfathers only care about our growing. They don't care about our getting a suntan, or acquiring a new car, or a new house, or a new job. Well, all right, they'll give us a new house or a new job if it is going to make us grow but they want us to *grow*, so, if we won't grow in the sunshine, they send the rain and the hail. They rain

149

us out, make it a little harder. So it's our own fault if we insist on growing through suffering. [laughter] We should grow through joy.

"And one of the most joyful things to me is the realization of all the new and old Medicine Wheels being reactivated or being created on the surface of this Turtle Island and in other places on our Mother Earth.

"One of the great Medicine Wheels of course, is Stonehenge. Another, the great rose mandala window in Notre Dame in Paris. And there are Medicine Wheels across Turtle Island. We came on one in Montana, fifteen hundred years old they said it was, which was discovered by the Crow people, and they were using it for a laboratory for astronomy...what is that thing called?...observatory. And the interesting thing is that the government— of what I call the counterculture, because I think that *we* are the culture [laughter and applause]— anyway, the counterculture had set up an observatory about two hundred yards away. Both things are working beautifully, though I rather think the Medicine Wheel one is more accurate. That's because I don't have a counterculture mathematical brain.

"But other Medicine Wheels are being set up everywhere. Small ones with people who don't have a back yard where they could put up a little bigger one. Small ones in the corner of the living room or a corner of the bedroom, to be covered by a beautiful cloth.

"And the purpose of these Medicine Wheels—of course, if you've read the great masterpiece of the age, which is my latest book—[much laughter] you'll *know* the meditation exercise on the Medicine Wheel. And the purpose, of course, is to use this great and wonderful—it's more than a tool—a companion in the work that a Medicine Wheel is.

"We've seen and participated in the setting up of this Medicine Wheel—Sun Bear's great and beautiful vision of how the Medicine Wheel should go and what we should be doing around it—but there are also other ways of using the Medicine Wheel.

"I'm thinking at the moment of the one we set up in Independence, in the Owens Valley, I should say. It's being used to try and reassure our Mother Earth that *some* of her children are remembering to return, and that we are trying to atone for and put back into Mother Earth tokens, at least, of some of the minerals and the mineral kingdom that have been raped from her, and taken away and used for wrong purposes.

"We're very conscious of the misuse of minerals where we live. Just over the hillside, on the other side of the valley in Nevada, they are continually doing underground and overground atomic tests. Every time they do an underground atomic test— we've had two this winter and they say there are ten more coming—the waters at Coso Hot Springs, which used to be a great healing place for the Paiutes, run radioactive twenty-four hours later. It travels underground. So our Mother Earth is being greatly polluted, greatly wounded and greatly harmed. And it is up to us, her children, to reverse the process of thousands of years when we've been taking, taking, taking, and try and put back.

151

"So this particular Medicine Wheel that I'm talking about, beautifully set up in a beautiful place, is used only for giving. We give, we give, we *give*. And we lay our hands, especially those of us who are healers, but everyone who goes there, on our Mother Earth. And treat her as we would a human patient, or an animal patient if we are holistic veterinarians...difficult thing to say...that I believe are coming into their own. We try and heal.

"It's like putting a Band-Aid on a very serious wound. But at least it is an intent. And we've seen signs of appreciation from the spirits of the valley and even from our Mother Earth that this token is being gratefully and graciously received. Like any mother when her child runs up with a treasure—a wilted flower or a little rock or something, always accepted as a wonderful present—our Mother Earth seems to be accepting our *belated* thanks, our belated gratitude and our belated attention as any mother does.

"So, I'm hoping that you will take back with you, all of you, some new things, some old things, very old things that you are actually going to *do*. It's no good hearing about all this, it's no good seeing these beautiful ceremonies, it's no good even taking part in them if you don't begin to *live* them.

"Absolutely the only thing that makes anything valid is: Is it *working*? Does it work and are we doing it? So I'm hoping that you will perhaps find a corner where you live to put up your own Medicine Wheel and meditate around it, and remember what happened in this one and think about what might happen in that one, and really use it.

"I'm also hoping that you're going to use smudging in your home, and in your place where you work, and in your cars, and in everything of importance to you. Lighten the vibrations with the sage and have a lot of fun doing it.

"Everyone, I think, is tired of my tale about what happened to me with a very nosy neighbor who came to see what this old woman was doing and saw me with my smudge pot around my car. He said, 'What are you doing?' Well, you have to tell the truth, but it needn't be the *relevant* truth. [much laughter] So I said, 'Termites!' [laughter] He was simply delighted and very smug. He thought, 'That old fool. She doesn't know that termites don't attack metal.' And I didn't enlighten him that I did know that. So we both parted very pleased with ourselves. [laughter]

"I dare you to introduce these things into your lives. If I can do it, you can. I'm talking to one woman who said what a horrible time she is having in her office. She hates her typewriter. I said, 'Have you smudged it?' She said, 'Oh, I could never do that.' I said, 'Why not? You could steal in there some lunch time and if you're overtaken you just say that it helps you to breathe.' Which it does, though not quite in the way they might think.

"If you can smudge the office, fine. If it's really impossible to do that, then you can do some mental exercises. You can speak to the typewriter. Typewriters are composed of metal and metal is alive. You can therefore say: 'Now look here, you! You're metal, you're all my relatives, yes. But I don't always love all my relatives. But I might

153

come to like you if you would behave yourself.'
[laughter]

"And one must, of course, talk to one's cells and
atoms in that way. [The sound of children shout-
ing in the background, marching past the audience, up a hill.]

"I think they're saying goodbye to us. Shall we
all go? You have to wait till you *leave* an assembly,
you see, to make sure everyone remembers. At
least for five minutes. [laughter]

"One should talk to one's atoms and cells. They
are sentient, intelligent beings. You talk to them as
you might to intelligent children. And you say,
'Now look here. My plan for us all working together is this kind of healthful body. My knee isn't
doing too well. See what you can do about that
....'You can talk to them like that with authority,
gentle but firm. If you can make them laugh, so
much the better.

"But then you come to your subconscious, and
you can't treat your subconscious in just the way
you treat your cells and atoms. You sort of sum-
mon your subconscious to a summit meeting.
[laughter] And you say, 'Now you know a lot of
things that I don't know. I know some things that
you don't know, and we're both involved in this
together. We're both in this human envelope, and
I want this kind of thing and I think you want the
same, don't you? [laughter] Let's work together
and get it.'

"A number of conversations like that and you'll
begin to see a difference in your whole being and
character.

"So I hope you'll go away with that feeling, and

154

the things that you've learned about yourselves and what we've learned about ourselves in these two days. Some of them beautiful things, some we'd rather not have to think about again.

"But we have to, we have to. Because there *is* an urgency about our graduating. This is a school. And here we are the Senior Class and we just refuse to graduate. [laughter]

"And here are all these persons waiting to come in and they can't because we've got all the desks. [Laughter, which obscures the next few words.]

"You know it's very disquieting, so what they're saying is, 'Pick up your feet. Graduate now.' And we're dragging our feet and we're saying, 'I don't want to do any more work. I think I'll drop out.'

"Well, it's not so easy to drop out of living, and if we do, we're making a terrible mistake....It simply means it takes us longer. Longer to graduate. We have free will, we can delay. But we can't avoid it. We have to graduate *some time or other*.

"And at this time, at the crossroads of our Mother Earth—I don't believe in the gloom and doom, the be-afraid school—our Mother Earth has gone through many, many evolutions. Many tiltings.

"Where I live near Death Valley, we can find... sharks' teeth and shells and every indication that it was once below the sea. You look at our mountains and they are volcanic and full of the most incredible formations that come from some gigantic upheaval. Our Mother Earth has gone through housekeeping many times. And emerged with a beautiful clean house.

"You know what it's like, housecleaning. Everybody wants to go away at once, dust flying every-where, you can't find anything, all your belong-ings are thrown out, or they're put away or something awful happens. But the net result is really rather pleasant when you come back to it.

"And I, for one, am looking forward to missing this, uhm, the housecleaning, a little bit, and coming back to it when it's all clean. [laughter] They may or may not let me get away with that.

"But at any rate, that's all it is. Housecleaning.

"What we *have* to stop is the man-made destruc-tion. The violence, the crime, the nuclear stuff, the greed, the corruption. And how do we stop that? We don't necessarily stop that by marching, or by saying it's terrible, or by turning off the television.

"We have to clean it up in ourselves. We have violence, we have greed, we have corruption. We have all these things in *here*. That's where it is. If we didn't, then there'd be nothing for these pro-grams coming in at us. But you see, these things don't come from us, they come *into* us and through us. The program of greed comes in, and suddenly you find you're being greedy. If we had nothing there that attracted it to us we would have turned that program off and turned on the oppo-site, of generosity.

"So we have to fight the enemy within. We are all warriors. Warriors of the rainbow. We have to fight the enemy inside us, and stop violence and greed and corruption and *fear* in the world by stop-ping it first in ourselves, and then in the people around us. If we can help them to see that and to do it, then it spreads. It spreads just as this won-

156

derful sharing of traditional knowledge has spread in the last few years.

"Do you suppose there were many gatherings like this a few years ago? Where our Indian traditional Medicine Men shared their most sacred, sacred and beautiful ceremonies with us, like the Pipe ceremony? Do you suppose there were many of those gatherings?

"And why are there some now? Because we have changed. We have grown a little. Enough to understand better. Enough to *want* to know better. Enough to want to live by these.

"So we go away from here, lots of lovely things to think about. And one small, minor thing. Not so minor when you come to think about it, and that is the food. The food was terrific. [applause] The people who have been feeding us, they were terrific. We need a hand for that.

"I'm drawing to a close of anything I have to say to you.

"I would like you to stand for a moment and to do the four affirmations. A very easy word that you can say in any language. The simple little word of YES.

"Great Spirit. Here we present ourselves to you, all that we are, all that we shall be when we soar shining. . . .

"Uniting with the blessed company of all faithful creatures, all our relatives throughout the worlds which you have made, and all those beings present, seen and unseen, we say yes, yes, yes, *yes* to your Divine Will for us and for all that you have made."

Nadine

It is finished in beauty. To a standing ovation, Evelyn Eaton slowly leaves the stage. When she reaches the platform steps she turns, and looking back at the audience, she calls out: "Go shining everyone! Go shining on your ways."

We publish books on:

Healing, Health and Diet ● Occultism and
Mysticism ● Transpersonal Psychology
Philosophy ● Religion ● Reincarnation
Theosophical Philosophy ● Yoga and Meditation

Other books of possible interest include:

Breath of the Invisible *by John Redtail Freesoul*
The spiritual heritage of the American Indian.

Children of the Rainbow *by Leinani Melville*
Long-kept secrets of the Hawaiian religion.

I Send a Voice *by Evelyn Eaton*
A white woman participates in Indian sweat lodge healings.

Imagineering for Health *by Serge King*
Self-healing through the use of the mind.

Kahuna Healing *by Serge King*
The holistic health practices of Polynesia.

The Shaman and the Medicine Wheel *by Evelyn Eaton*
A first-person account of American Indian healing rituals.

Shamanism *compiled by Shirley Nicholson*
Describes how these old, world-wide spiritual practices work.

A Still Forest Pool *edited by J. Kornfield & P. Breiter*
Living philosophy of Achaan Chah, great forest master.

Available from:
The Theosophical Publishing House
306 W. Geneva Road, Wheaton, Illinois 60187